Arctic Fever

Clarke, Irwin & Company Limited/TORONTO/VANCOUVER/1971

Arctic Fever: The Search for the Northwest Passage

BY DOUG WILKINSON

To Cezar Heine
a very good friend in a time of need.
Yellowknife, N.W.T. 1972

Doug Wilkinson

© 1971 by Clarke, Irwin & Company Limited
Printed in Canada
ISBN 0-7720-0504-4

1 2 3 4 5 6 JD 76 75 74 73 72 71

In every age there have been men who took "one small step for man, one giant step for mankind." This book is about men who took giant steps across the Arctic region of North America, in the years before the Canadian nation came into being.

To the wives of the explorers, about whom we hear little, but to whom we owe much, this book is dedicated.

Prologue

The age of geographic discovery on earth is over; no longer does man dream of unknown lands that lie beyond distant horizons. During hundreds of years of cautious probing into all corners of the globe man has traced the jagged outline of the continents, pinpointed the position of the islands in the seas, plotted the course of rivers and lakes until the surface features of the entire world are as well-known to him as the paths of his own woods, the far corners of his tilled fields, the streets of his city or town. In the late twentieth century, man no longer looks to the earthly horizon of sea and sky. His gaze is set straight up, to the planets and the stars, and he wonders what he may find out there in the vastness of unexplored space. Today we live in the dawn of a new era of exploration, and explorers, which will see men and machines rocket out from earth to probe the utmost limits of our system of planets, and perhaps beyond this into the unspeakably vast distances of outer space.

Still, there will be exploration on earth, by explorers who will never leave the terrestial globe. As British geographer, the late George Debenham, wrote in 1932:

> ... discovery in the geographical sense will soon be a thing of the past, for we shall shortly know, at least in outline, the main geographical features of every part of the world. But exploration—the detailed examination of unfrequented tracts

—is likely to provide work for geographical pioneers for the next century or longer.*

In Canada we live with one of the earth's "unfrequented tracts" at our back door. How fortunate we are to have such a huge area of land, lake and sea where it is still possible to stand on ground trod by no human foot before. How fortunate we are to have on our national doorstep places from which we can look out over bush, tundra or sea and know that the nearest neighbour is 200 miles away. How fortunate we are to be able to follow many trails of early explorers and see our land much as it must have looked to their eyes so long ago.

Explorer! A powerful word, evoking pictures of valiant men performing great deeds and heroic actions in distant lands that lie beyond the boundaries of the cosy world in which most of mankind lives; speaking of men of courage and vision who, struggling against fearful odds, sometimes winning, sometimes losing, seek to roll back the known limits of the earth.

Arctic! Another powerful word which conjures up images of glacial ice and snow, of six months' darkness followed by six months' daylight, of northern lights that sweep and crackle across frosty, star-filled skies, of lands forlorn at the top of the world.

Arctic explorers! Men afflicted with that strange malady, Arctic fever, for which there is no cure but to put the patient on ice.

* J. Mirsky, *To the Arctic* (New York: Alfred A. Knopf, 1948).

Contents

Acknowledgements

Of ice and sailing ships: Overleaf: Metropolitan Toronto Library Board, A and B: Public Archives of Canada, C and D and E: Metropolitan Toronto Library Board

The explorer as artist: B and C and D: Metropolitan Toronto Library Board

The explorer as artist (continued): A and B and C and D: Metropolitan Toronto Library Board, E: British Museum

The two documents: A: National Maritime Museum, B: Public Archives of Canada

Old and new: Overleaf: National Film Board, A: National Film Board, B: Department of Transport, C and D and E: National Film Board

Twentieth-century man comes to the Arctic: B: National Film Board, D: Department of Transport, E: Canadian Army Photo

Doug Wilkinson in the Arctic: C: National Film Board

Modern communication and transportation: A: National Defence Photograph, B: National Film Board

Map: The Beaver and Colonel Baird

Photo of author on jacket: National Film Board

Front of jacket: Public Archives of Canada

The four portraits: Public Archives of Canada

Arctic Fever

The Chimera

On a clear crisp day in July 1960, I sat in the cramped front seat of my Piper Super Cub cruising westward at 2,000 feet over the coast of lower Boothia Peninsula, the most northerly extension of the North American continent. An hour before I had taken off from the tiny sand beach of an island in front of the Roman Catholic mission at Pelly Bay and turned due west, climbing for altitude enroute to the Arctic settlement of Gjoa Haven on King William Island. The aircraft rode rock-steady in the smooth air. Only the sharp, intermittent crackle of static in the headphones of the high frequency radio disturbed the serenity of the day.

This short flight along the north central coast of Canada wasn't much different from dozens of other such flights made in previous years, nor from the hundreds flown since that date, except for one thing. That day I was going to fly over an Arctic sea channel that I had not seen before in summer, one I had been waiting to see for over fifteen years. In those years I had travelled almost every coast of the Canadian Arctic mainland and the northern islands. By dogs and sled I had trekked hundreds of miles over the sea ice of Hudson Bay and the inlets of north Baffin Island. On board Peterhead boats I had hunted walrus, seals and polar bears in Frozen Strait and Roes Welcome Sound. On small supply ships I had sailed along the great water gateways of Hudson Strait and Lancaster Sound. I had been on board icebreakers as they fought their way through the massive floes of Foxe Basin and Baffin Bay. In my small plane I had crossed and recrossed almost every Arctic sea lane, right up to Robeson Channel and the Arctic Ocean off northern Ellesmere Island.

But there was one tiny section of Arctic coast that I wanted to see in summer, and it had eluded me until that July day in 1960. As I looked down at the dull brown landscape sliding past beneath the fat, balloon tires of the plane an ever-mounting sense of excitement sent small shivers down my spine.

The Cub passed over the DEW[1] Line Site at Shepherd Bay and I reported, by station, on flight plan. All was well. The coast skimmed beneath as the plane flew out over the water-covered ice of a small bay. Up ahead I could see the low outline of Cape Colville, and beyond—there it was—the open water of Rae Strait, green and blue, dappled with short, choppy waves, its surface dotted with myriad pieces of drifting white ice. The plane droned on while I gazed down in wonder.

Rae Strait? You've never heard of it!

Come to think of it, if you haven't, there's good reason. It isn't much of a body of water. It can't begin to compare with the northern majesty of Hudson Strait or Lancaster Sound. Rae Strait is short, narrow and shallow. Even on maps where it is identified the name tends to get swallowed up in the welter of names around. It lacks the sense of history that surrounds better known Fury and Hecla Strait, or Bellot Strait off the northern tip of the North American mainland. But don't be misled by this apparent insignificance; Rae Strait was once the most sought after sea channel in the entire western world. It was the key to the Northwest Passage seaway across the top of North America, the chimera that, century after century, sent men and

[1] Distant Early Warning

ships from most European nations on a ceaseless quest of geographic discovery that has no parallel in all recorded history.

A Northwest Passage to Asia—dream of bold men for 400 years. The search for it began in the sixteenth century but the passage wasn't sailed until the beginning of the twentieth. To spur its discovery nations offered cash rewards, as well as grants of exclusive trade and commerce in all lands along its route to whomsoever should be the first to pass by sea from Atlantic to Pacific, or vice versa, across the top of the North American continent. Century after century Portugal, Spain, France, Holland, Norway and England all sent men and ships west and north to seek out this missing link in the sea routes of the world. England alone spent millions of pounds, lost dozens of ships and hundreds of men seeking the elusive waterway. Bit by bit, over 400 years, a passage was discovered, and the last link to be sailed was Rae Strait.

For a better look I let down to 500 feet, something I do only rarely while flying over open water on wheels in the Arctic. But this was a special occasion and I took the risk gladly. There, so close beneath my plane, were the waters of Rae Strait, as they must have looked to Amundsen when he sailed through here in 1903—the first European to navigate the passage by ship. They must have looked this way on a July day in 1848 as the survivors of Franklin's last expedition, after searching in vain for this tiny waterway, were struggling south to their ghastly deaths from starvation only a few miles from where I flew. They must have looked like this on a July day in 1611 as, far off to the southeast, Henry Hudson was being set adrift by members of his mutinous crew after failing to find the passage he so assiduously sought.

One of the members of Hudson's original crew was named Wilkinson. Now, another Wilkinson sailed the Northwest Passage, flying swiftly and easily in his ship of the air, looking down with eager eyes at this little-known channel that had lured so many men into the unknown dangers of Arctic Canada. The

Arctic explorers had come from many nations, from many walks of life. They did not know what they would discover in this land of snow and ice and water. They did not know, but they believed.

They believed that a sea channel across the top of America existed, that it would lead them to Asia and the Far East, and that God has so arranged His affairs that they would be its discoverers. On such belief they were willing to risk all—their reputations, their fortunes, their lives. They did not know, could not know, that they had set as their task the most arduous, dangerous and difficult task of geographic discovery that the world has ever known. The history of its undertaking reads as one great sorrow. In the words of Fridtjof Nansen, an outstanding Arctic explorer:

> The history of Polar exploration is a single, mighty manifestation of the power of the unknown over the mind of man, perhaps greater and more evident here than in any other phase of human life. Nowhere else in the world have we won our way so slowly; nowhere else has every new step caused so much trouble, so many privations and sufferings; and certainly nowhere have the resulting discoveries promised fewer material advantages.
>
> And nevertheless, new forces have always been found ready to carry the attack further, to stretch once more the limits of the world.[2]

[2] Fridtjof Nansen, *In Northern Mists* (London: W. Heinemann, 1911 and New York: F. A. Stokes, 1911), p. 4.

Journey to Baffin Island

Montreal International Airport: the high pitched scream of arriving and departing jets echoes across the tarmac and through the busy terminal. CP Air Flight 72 from Vancouver, Air Canada 870 off for Germany, BOAC departing for London, Eastern Airlines in from Miami. East, west and south the huge aircraft go and come, carrying hundreds of passengers on effortless trips to the far corners of the globe.

From the concrete surface of Runway 24 a gleaming Boeing 737 jet rises steeply, sun reflecting from the white insignia on the blue tail. Nordair Flight No. 709, northbound to Frobisher Bay on southern Baffin Island, climbs swiftly, then banks right, until it is headed almost due north. In a few minutes it has left behind the patterned fields of the St. Lawrence valley and is flying high over the seemingly endless expanse of the sub-Arctic Canadian bush. Thirty thousand feet below, bush and lake drift lazily by, country of Indian trapper and French-Canadian lumberjack. Two hours out of Montreal the bush begins to peter out, replaced by the ice-dotted waters of Ungava Bay. The steep rock cliffs of Akpatok Island, rising 1,000 feet sheer out the Bay, drift slowly beneath the starboard wing. Beyond is Hudson Strait, its deep blue surface dotted with white patches of scattered ice floes and solitary ice-bergs. A long line of black smoke points to the position of a grain boat inbound for Churchill on Hudson Bay.

A slight popping in the ears announces that the plane is slowly letting down over southern Baffin Island. No bush here, just barren, rocky, still snow-covered coast stretching east and west as far as the eye can see. On the maps this land is called "Meta Incognita"[1]—so named by Queen Elizabeth I in 1577 (somewhat prophetically in view of future events on Baffin Island). Not quite three hours after leaving Montreal, 1,100 miles away to the south, the jet plops hard onto the long black runway of the airport at the Arctic town of Frobisher Bay.

Frobisher Bay is the territorial government administrative centre for the Eastern Arctic. With its 1,500 inhabitants, its huge airfield, its new hotel and high-rise apartment, its shopping centre and dozens of small houses, it is the largest and most modern town anywhere north of the tree line in Canada. The sights and sounds of the town are the same as those in any developing community: trucks and buses rumble over the gravel roads, jackhammers pound, diesel engines roar. Although there are no trees, no flowers, no grass and although huge pieces of sea ice float back and forth in the harbour, the general look, feel and mood of the town is late-twentieth century, with all the good and bad that implies.

But drive up the steep, winding road that leads to the abandoned radar station and you begin to leave the twentieth century behind. Park your car and walk over the hill. The town disappears, the sounds die away. Before you is a long valley hemmed between walls of broken black rock, carpeted with fields of long grass, cut by shallow streams that dance and bubble their way over smooth stones towards the distant sea. White heads of Arctic Cotton Grass dance in the stiff breeze, the yellow of Arctic Poppies reflects the summer sun, the air is filled with the buzz of hundreds of mosquitoes. Small birds flit

[1] Unknown goal

low over the tundra, a coal-black raven glides by croaking harshly as it disappears over a ridge of rock. Slowly your head turns as your eyes wander over the land. You are alone, on Baffin Island, looking out over landscape that has not changed much in the past 5,000 years.

Take a trip by small boat down Frobisher Bay. The tide is full and your big freighter canoe swings away from the shore, well clear of the rocks that lie beneath. In half an hour all signs of man have disappeared. Again you are alone: only you and your guide moving swiftly by lonely islets, past massive pieces of intricately sculptured sea ice. A seal's head breaks the smooth surface of the sea; shoe-button eyes watch warily from afar. A gull rises lazily from a lichen-covered rock near the shore and wings gracefully away towards the land. The sound of the outboard echoes back from high rock cliffs that have looked down over these waters for thousands of years, as they will continue to look down for thousands of years into the future.

A small island appears ahead of the canoe. You glide in towards the shore and the hum of the outboard motor dies away. The only sound is the soft lapping of water under the bow as the canoe slips up to the rocky shore. Above your head rises a long gravel bank and, cut through the bank, is a V-shaped notch, several feet deep, running straight inland for a dozen yards and more. The trench looks unnatural, and so it is, cut by human hands almost 400 years ago. This is the dry dock dug by sailors of Martin Frobisher in the year 1578 so they could drag their wooden sailing ships out of the water and repair the ice damaged hulls.

> . . . our ships, even those of the greatest burdens, were heaved up between Islands of yce, a foote welneere out of the sea above their watermarke, having their knees and timbers within boord bowed, and broken therewith.[2]

[2] Richard Hakluyt, *The Principall Navigations, Voiages and Discoveries of the English Nation* (London, 1589), Vol. VII, p. 331.

Clamber slowly up the trench as you wonder about these Englishmen long since dead. What must have been their thoughts as they hauled their ships from the ice-filled seas out onto the treeless, barren land to which they had come?

. . . here, in place of odiferous and fragrant smels of sweete gums, and pleasant notes of musicall birds, which other Counteys in more temperate Zones do yeeld, wee tasted the most boisterous Boreal blasts mixt with snow and haile, in the months of June and July.[3]

Walk to the edge of one of the deep pits dug by these same mariners who thought they had landed in Asia, and who thought the rocks they dug from these pits were gold.

. . . the stones of this supposed continent with America, be altogether sparkeld, and glisten in the sunne like gold; so likewise doth the sand in the bright water, yet they verifie the old Proverb: All is not gold that Glitereth.[4]

Search carefully and you will see the faint outline of the small house they built.

. . . of lime and stone to the end that we might prove against our return whether the snow could overwhelm it, the frost to break it up, or the country people to dismember it. And the better to allay these brutish and uncivil people of this land we left therein divers of our countries toys.[5]

Glance up at the man standing beside you, who has brought you to this lonely spot. He is a direct descendant of the "brutish and uncivil" people who first met men from western Europe on the shores of Frobisher Bay.

[3] *Ibid.*, p. 214.
[4] *Ibid.*, pp. 218-19.
[5] *Ibid.*, p. 362.

... being ashore on the top of a hill he perceived a number of small things fleeting in the sea afarre off, which he supposed to be porposes or seales, or some kind of strange fish; but coming neere, he discovered them to be men in small boats made of leather . . . . they came aboard his ship, and brought him salmon and raw flesh and fish, and greedily devoured the same before our men's faces. . . . they exchanged coats of seales, and beares skinnes, and such like with our men; and received belles, looking glasses, and other toyes in recompense thereof againe. After great courtesie, and many greetings, our mariners, contrary to their Captaines direction, began more easily to trust them; and five of our men going ashore were by them intercepted in their boat, and were never since heard of to this day againe.[6]

On the shores of Frobisher Bay you stand on historic ground. All about are the signs of people who passed this way long ago—the English, the Eskimos, and other men from an even more remote and ancient past. Walk west from the town of Frobisher Bay, past the airfield and the oil storage tanks, over the rocky ridge to the banks of the Sylvia Grinnell River. Here you will find piles of jumbled stones, fish caches built by Eskimo hunters who took Arctic char from the river mouth 600 years ago. And, if you search carefully over the gravel beaches nearby, you will find tiny chipped stones called burins, cutting implements left behind by still earlier fishermen who camped on this site 5,000 years ago.

* *Ibid.*, pp. 280-1.

Arctic Wanderers

Three thousand years before the birth of Christ, men first laid eyes on the waters of what is now Frobisher Bay. Out of Asia they had come, Paleolithic hunters well adapted to life in the Arctic cold. They were not Eskimos in the modern sense but they had an Eskimo-like way of life. Completely unknown to other men who were slowly developing complex civilizations in the valleys of the Nile, the Euphrates, the Ganges and the Yangtze rivers in the Old World, these early Arctic hunters lived in small widely-scattered groups, moving about with the change of season, harvesting the animals of land and sea on which they depended for their food, their clothing and their shelter. Gradually they drifted along the northern sea coasts until they occupied all the lands around the rim of the Arctic Ocean.

Until about 800 B.C. these Arctic nomads, called Pre-Dorset people by science, hunted over the water and ice-covered sea off the north coast of Canada along the entire route of the Northwest Passage waterway. They hunted the waters off northern North America for seals, walrus and polar bears. To the early Arctic hunters this far north land was something special: it was their home and they probably loved it equally as much as do Eskimo hunters of more modern times. There is a tale told in the far north of an Eskimo hunter who so loved his homeland that he rarely left it. Only once was he persuaded to leave, to go away on a long sled journey. When he returned and climbed the hill back of his campsite to sit and gaze out over the vista of ice and snow-covered rock that he knew so well, his heart swelled up and burst. He died of happiness.

Gradually, over many centuries, the way of life of the Pre-Dorset hunters underwent change and modification to settle into a new pattern which we call Dorset culture. The Dorsets, like their predecessors, lived in small groups as nomadic hunters, using skin tents for shelter in the short summer, and pit-type houses covered over with a roof of skins during the long winter. Dorset hunters probably invented and perfected the snow house, or igloo as it has come to be called, that classic example of simplicity and efficiency of design and construction which required only materials that lay at hand in an Arctic land.

Dorset men hunted seals, walrus, caribou. They speared fish at the stone weirs on the rivers. Dorset women fashioned tailored clothing from the skins of the animals killed by their husbands and sons, sewing in their tents and houses by the light of small, blubber-burning, soapstone lamps. The Dorsets didn't have dogs; they man-hauled their meagre possessions on small, wooden sleds with runners shod with ivory. They were the greatest foot-travellers the world has ever known. Over hundreds of centuries Pre-Dorset and Dorset men, women and children walked from northern Asia halfway around the world to Greenland. At least 4,000 years before M'Clure, Amundsen and Larsen, they had travelled the Northwest Passage across the top of the American continent.

About A.D. 900, at the time when the early Norse were settling in Iceland and beginning their sea voyages to Greenland and eastern North America, at the time when Alfred the Great was defeating the Danes at Salisbury Plain to lay the foundations of Anglo-Saxon England from which modern Britain sprang, a thin wave of immigrants of an Arctic culture different from that of the Dorsets began to sweep swiftly across the north coast of Canada. There are two conflicting views as to the origin of this new group of northern people, one firmly rooted in the minds of most scholars who have devoted much of their lives to the study of man and his movements in the far north; the other, more novel, more romantic, but seriously proposed by a few, equally knowledgeable men.

The orthodox view is that hunters of the Thule culture, as the newcomers have been called, like the original Arctic people, came out of Asia. By A.D. 1000 they had reached the area of Rae Strait on the north central coast of Canada. By A.D. 1100 they were on Baffin Island and Greenland. Almost everywhere they replaced the Dorsets. Most Thule people were classic Eskimos—in their adaptation to an Arctic land, in their language, in their physical appearance. Although they hunted seals, walrus, caribou and fish, using techniques not unlike those of the Dorset people they replaced, Thule Eskimos evolved further by developing and perfecting a technique for hunting big whales on the sea. This gave them a major source of food, fuel and building material quite beyond the capabilities of the Dorsets.

These advantages allowed them to live in expanded winter villages that commonly contained up to thirty-five large houses, each made from slabs of stone and sod set over a framework of large whalebones. The Thule house, partly underground and set into a gentle slope facing out onto the sea, was a large, comfortable winter dwelling with a subterranean entrance, a raised sleeping platform of flagstones, a flagstone floor, and stone "cupboards" for the storage of food and clothing.[1]

---

[1] Many years ago I stayed in a Thule house on north Baffin Island where I was living as the adopted "son" of an Eskimo hunter. Neighbours of ours had reached their winter campground too late in the season to build a new house of sod and skin so they roofed over a long-abandoned Thule house, one of many in this area. I stayed only one night in the house, but found it, heated by two small seal-oil lamps and eight bodies, to be warm and comfortable. The only unusual feature were the mice that scampered about among the nooks and crannies of the flagstone walls.

Thule people had domesticated dogs and they used them for hunting and for hauling their sleds, thus increasing the range of their movements and the speed at which they could travel. This is evident in the swiftness of their spread across the entire range of Arctic lands in the western hemisphere.

They invented a huge skin boat, the umiak, made of walrus or square-flipper seal hides sewn over a wooden frame. This they used for their whale hunts, and to transport all their possessions, as well as their women and children, along the water routes of the Northwest Passage.

The other theory of the origin of the Thule Eskimos is quite different. A few scholars believe them to be the result of an intermixture between invading Norse, from the "lost" colonies in Greenland, and the Dorset Eskimos. There is some sound evidence to support this view. Many of the early whalers and explorers in Arctic Canada wrote about the distinctly European facial and body features of some of the Eskimos they met. Some even went so far as to state flatly that they believed the Eskimos they met to be of two different groups.

As early as 1615 the English captain of a fishing vessel operating in Baffin Bay described how he met people who seemed to be of two distinct types—one group tall, fair, well-proportioned; the other smaller, with short legs and a dark complexion. In 1837 Thomas Simpson described Eskimos he met on the north central coast as having a distinguished appearance, much like Scandinavians. In 1910 the modern Arctic explorer, Vihjalmur Stefansson, first heard about "blond" Eskimos from members of the crew of a whaling ship that had wintered at Banks Island. He journeyed to Victoria Island and lived with a group of people who had never before met a European. The following passage is his diary entry for May 16, 1910.

I now understand why the Cape Bexley people (the first Eskimos discovered by us) take me for an Eskimo. There are three men here whose beards are almost the color of mine, and who look like typical Scandinavians. . . . Here (in Victoria

Island) . . . are men with abundant three inch beards, a light brown in their outer parts, but darker toward the middle of the chin. The faces and proportions of the body remind me of "stocky," sunburned, but naturally fair, Scandinavians.[2]

More recently the late Professor Tryggvi Oleson, in his book *Early Voyages and Northern Approaches,* outlined his belief in a European ancestry for Thule Eskimos. His thesis is based on references in the Icelandic Sagas, on the accounts of early explorers, on archaeological evidence, and on Eskimo legends which tell of the Tunit, a race of giants living on the north coast. He presents a persuasive case, one not yet accepted by many scholars, but one with broad appeal to the romanticist. Who could resist the thought that modern Eskimos of northern Canada are descended from early Eskimo hunters and men of the Viking race from the "lost" colonies on Greenland?

Whatever their origin, to the Thule Eskimo hunters the Northwest Passage across the top of America was no mystery. Whether they came to it from east or west they knew its ice and open water intimately.

At the time Thule hunters were spreading along the Northwest Passage, the weather in the far north began to turn colder than it had for centuries past. Out from their mountain fastness the glaciers of the high Arctic islands flowed to cover much of the lower land again. Ice cover on the sea became more extensive. The open water season grew shorter. In places there was no longer any open water in the summer. Lacking this, the big whales no longer appeared in the sea channels between the islands. Most Thule hunters were forced to abandon their lucrative whale hunts, to leave their large winter villages and become increasingly nomadic. They lived in snow houses on the sea-ice surface in winter, and in tents made from skins in the short summer.

[2] Vilhjalmur Stefansson, *My Life with the Eskimo* (New York: The Macmillan Company, 1927), p. 205.

Gradually they developed a new way of life based on the hunting of seals: through the breathing holes in the ice in winter, on the surface of the ice in spring, and from skin-covered kayaks on the restricted open water channels in summer. They continued to fish at weirs on the rivers, and to hunt caribou on the land back of the coasts in the autumn. A few groups left the sea coast entirely to live inland among the immense herds of caribou in what is now the District of Keewatin. But most stayed by the sea. On the north central coast of Canada, from Baffin Island through to the mouth of the Mackenzie River, they developed and perfected their distinctive seal-hunt culture. They are the direct ancestors of the modern Eskimos, and many of their descendants hunt and travel over the ice of the Northwest Passage waterway to this day.

Unfortunately the seal-hunt culture was destined to last for an even shorter period of time than had the life based on the hunting of whales. Even as groups of hunters along the north central coast from Pelly Bay to Coppermine were bringing seal-hunt techniques to a peak of development and refinement, their brothers on Baffin Island were beginning to witness the arrival on their shores of the latest group of men to come to Arctic America. It was a party of hunters from an outpost of Thule Eskimos who, in the year 1576, came out in their kayaks to greet the Englishman, Martin Frobisher, when he sailed into his bay.

Across the North Atlantic

On the morning of the 7th of June, 1576, three small sailing ships moved slowly down the river Thames, heading for the North Sea and the north Atlantic Ocean. Almost immediately the smallest of the ships, a tiny pinnace, got into difficulties. She collided with an anchored ship, smashing her bowsprit and foremast. The three ships were forced to anchor while repairs were made to the damaged pinnace, and it wasn't until the next day that they weighed anchor again to resume their journey. From the window of her palace at Greenwich, Queen Elizabeth waved a brief farewell, to which the ships replied by firing a salute from a cannon. Martin Frobisher was off to find a northern sea route to Asia.

Frobisher's ships—the twenty-ton *Gabriel*, especially built for the venture; the twenty-five-ton *Michael*; and a pinnace of only seven tons—were tiny vessels. The *Gabriel* was about the size of a modern ship's lifeboat. The combined tonnage of all three was less than that of the soon-to-be famous *Mayflower*. None were well-suited to the voyage that lay ahead, but to Martin Frobisher, frustrated through ten years of attempting to interest backers in the feasibility of a Northwest Passage, they were better than nothing.

Because Frobisher's vessels were small, unwieldy and slow we tend to think of them as being ill-equipped and poorly provisioned for the sea voyage they were about to undertake. We tend to think of the men who manned the ships as intrepid, but lacking in training and knowledge for their appointed task. Nothing could be further from the truth. Frobisher's ships carried nearly ten tons of food, and pots and pans in which to cook it. The food may not have been as appetizing or nutritious as ship's stores today but it was standard for the mid-seventeenth century—salted and dried meat, and ship's biscuits.

Frobisher had on board his flagship, the *Gabriel*, the most modern navigation equipment then available—compasses, hour glass, cross-stall and astrolabe. His supply of maps and charts of the world, as it was known at the time, was the best available. There was even a small library of books on previous voyages of discovery. Prior to the voyage Frobisher and his ship's officers had been given detailed geographic and scientific instruction by Dr. John Dee, a gifted mathematician and astrologer. Unfortunately, the relatively unschooled Frobisher was to find that much of the written instruction supplied by Dr. Dee was mathematically away over his head.

It was late in June before adverse head winds allowed the little fleet to get clear of the English coast. By this time the *Michael* was leaking badly and Frobisher was forced to seek harbour in the Shetland Isles in order to repair the worst of the leaks and to refill the fresh-water casks. Early in July the ships left harbour and sailed due west across the North Atlantic. Although battered by a series of early storms, during one of which the tiny pinnace and its three-man crew vanished never to be seen again, the *Gabriel* and *Michael* made good progress. Their plotted course must have been along the sixtieth degree of latitude for, on July 11th, the lookout sighted land. Far off their starboard bow rose the southern tip of Greenland. As they drew closer Frobisher saw the rocky headland rising up "like pinnacles of steeples, and all covered with snow."[1] He was the

[1] Richard Hakluyt, *The Principall Navigations . . .* , p. 206.

first European to see this coast since the Norse had found and then lost it 200 years before.

Frobisher tried hard to bear in on this forbidding coast to land and explore, but fields of heavy sea ice, studded with icebergs, kept his ships well off shore. He was forced to haul away without effecting a landing. Then, on the 13th of July disaster struck. Almost without warning the ships were hit by the worst storm they had experienced so far. As the waves rose and the wind howled out of the north, the *Michael* disappeared from view.[2] The storm increased in violence. Immense waves tossed the *Gabriel* unmercifully. Violent winds tore through the tattered sail and rigging. Suddenly the ship was thrown flat on her side in the raging sea. Tons of dark green water poured into the open centre section. With their ship flat on the sea and seemingly about to founder, the crew panicked. To the terrified seamen it seemed like the end of the world. Here was a situation to bring out the worst, or the best, in a man.

Martin Frobisher proved equal to the challenge. In fact, he seems to have delighted in any struggle with the odds against him. Using his great strength he clambered forward along the side of the wildly tossing vessel and managed to release the foresail halyard, thus relieving some of the pressure that was keeping the ship on its side in the raging sea. The foreyard snapped off and the main top mast broke away. Some members of the crew were about to chop away the mainmast as well but Frobisher managed to stop them. Without the mainmast they would have been derelict on the sea.

Slowly the ship came upright again. With her open deck full of water she wallowed helplessly, unable to answer to the helm. As wave after wave swept over her, Frobisher rallied his men. For a whole day they pumped furiously while the ship drifted free before the wind, every man expecting each moment might be his last. But the ship held together, the pumps slowly gained on the water, and gradually the winds died down. The *Gabriel*

---

[2] The *Michael* weathered the storm but returned to England to report the *Gabriel* lost with all hands.

still floated but she was badly battered, in desperate need of repair.

Through all the difficulties Frobisher never once thought of turning for home. Despite the loss of the pinnace, and then the *Michael*; despite the sad condition of the *Gabriel* and the mutterings of his dispirited crew, he pushed his ship westward, trying to reach the coast of Labrador so that he could get to shore and repair the damage caused by the storm. He reassured the crew that "the sea at length must needs have an endynge."[3] For two weeks the battered ship crept slowly westward until, on July 29th, Frobisher himself was the first to site land ahead, a high, rocky headland rising out of an ice-filled sea. Frobisher named it Queen Elizabeth's Foreland, in honour of his patron Queen. The *Gabriel* had reached an island off the southeast corner of Baffin Island just north of the entrance to what is now Frobisher Bay.

The *Gabriel* was leaking badly. Frobisher had to get the ship on shore. But great ice fields blocked the coast as far as he could see and for days he was forced to beat up and down the forbidding shoreline searching for an opening into the land. All the while his crew manned the pumps continuously. Gradually the ice broke up and drifted away. An opening appeared and Frobisher managed to beach the *Gabriel* on a tidal flat where the crew made temporary repairs.

On August 11th, almost two months after the departure from England, the *Gabriel* floated free on a rising tide and once more set out for the northwest. Down the long reach of Frobisher Bay she sailed in completely unknown waters now, impeded only by scattered patches of drifting ice around which Frobisher manoeuvred the ship with ease. On his left was a high, rock-bound coast mantled with glacial ice that glistened in the summer sun. On his right was a lower, but equally rocky coast with hilltops cloaked in patches of low cloud that clung, ghost-like, on the upper slopes.

[3] Hakluyt, *The Principall Navigations* . . . , p. 279.

Frobisher was overjoyed. His earlier misfortunes were all but forgotten. For 150 miles he sailed his ship steadily westward, moving easily among the towering pieces of drift ice that moved back and forth with wind and tide. He was sure this channel was the Northwest Passage to the fabled land of Cathay, that the high land on his left was the North American continent, that the coast on his right was a long extension of Asia. As Magellan had found a passage at the southern tip of South America and called it Magellan's Strait, so Martin Frobisher thought he had found a passage around the north of North America, and he called his passage "Frobisher's Streightes."[4]

On the north side of the "strait" Frobisher landed on a small island in order to take observations. He could see nothing but scattered islands and open water to the west. As he scanned the water with his glass he saw what he took to be a school of porpoises swimming towards the shore of the little cove in which he had landed. To his amazement the porpoises turned out to be men, strange creatures dressed in skins of seals, paddling small boats made of seals' skins. Martin Frobisher had become the first Englishman to meet Eskimos in the Canadian north. He watched amazed and fascinated as the Eskimos manoeuvred their kayaks among the floating ice hummocks, moving steadily towards the shore.

Suddenly he shouted. Amazement was quickly replaced by consternation, for the Eskimos appeared to be trying to cut Frobisher and his men off from their boat. Pell-mell down the slope they ran, reaching the boat ahead of the Eskimos in their kayaks. With great haste they pushed off and rowed quickly back to the *Gabriel* where everything was put in readiness for a possible attack. In the sixteenth century every strange ship was treated as an enemy until proven otherwise, even a skin-covered kayak.

The Eskimos made no move to attack. Emboldened by this, Frobisher sent some of his crew in the small boat to meet and

4 *Ibid.*, p. 215.

talk with them while he stood guard on the *Gabriel*. By signs the Eskimos showed themselves to be friendly. One man was enticed to come on board the *Gabriel*, but only after one of the seamen volunteered to remain as hostage with the remaining Eskimos. Once on board the Eskimo hunter looked about in wonder at the huge ship, touching this, stroking that, his eyes and manner expressing his bewilderment and, eventually, his joy at everything he saw. Frobisher gave the man some ship's meat and a mug of wine, neither of which the Eskimo liked very much for he made wry faces at the taste of both. But he had lost all fear of the ship and its crew and soon all the Eskimos were on board, examining, touching, exclaiming in wonder. They clambered over the vessel examining it from top to bottom. Into the rigging they climbed, first to imitate the movements of the sailors and then to perform acrobatics and stunts of their own before the eyes of the appreciative crew. They were persuaded to exchange sealskins and bearskins for combs and cups, mirrors and brightly coloured beads.

Martin Frobisher's heart must have been filled with joy on that day. Behind him lay ten years of dreaming, and two months of hardship and toil. Before him lay an open-water channel that led off to the west. He was sure he had discovered the Northwest Passage that would lead him direct to the rich lands of the Far East. He believed the land on which he had gone ashore was a part of Asia. Even the features of the people he had met confirmed this—round faces, high cheekbones, slightly slanted eyes, like the Tartars of the East. How sweet life must have seemed to Martin Frobisher at that moment. His troubles were over; all he had to do was sail west to Cathay, and to wealth and honour when he returned to England.

Immediately he made his plans to start west. From a high hill he could see two prominent headlands far down the "strait" and he judged these to mark its western end. Beyond must lie the open sea. In return for a bell and a knife, one of the Eskimos was persuaded to guide the *Gabriel* past the island in the strait.

The Eskimo seemed to indicate that it would take two days to reach the sea beyond.

Frobisher sent the Eskimo ashore to get his kayak and gear. However, in spite of the apparent friendliness of the native people, Frobisher was still wary. He instructed his boat crew to land the man on a point of land some distance from his camp on shore, and then return to the ship immediately. He watched as the crew followed his orders. The boat pulled in and the Eskimo jumped ashore. The boat pushed off again but, to Frobisher's amazement, it didn't start back towards the ship. Pulling lustily the crew rowed off along the rocky shore, away from the *Gabriel*, until they were lost to view around a rocky headland. After a few moments the boat reappeared farther down the bay but now there were only two men in it. They rowed around a rocky point and were lost to view.

Frobisher was furious. This was mutiny. He had lost five men from his small crew and he had lost his only boat. Without the boat he would not be able to work his way among the channels that lay ahead, nor could he get from the ship to the shore. He ordered the *Gabriel* to sail back and forth firing the cannon, while he sounded blasts on the trumpet. But there was no sign of his men or of the Eskimos. He thought he heard laughter coming from behind the rocks on shore and this angered him even further. He resolved to try to take Eskimo prisoners in order to barter for the return of his men.

For three days he sailed the shores of the bay searching for Eskimos, but found none. Returning to the place where his men had vanished he found no sign of Eskimos there. The *Gabriel* and its crew of thirteen men were alone. What a change a few days had made. Even a man of such strong personality as Frobisher must have felt the tug of despair. He was so close to the realization of his dreams; so close; so close.

Suddenly there came a shout from one of his crew. Ahead of the ship appeared a small flotilla of boats, an umiak loaded with Eskimo men and women, and ten kayaks each with a single hunter, each man armed with bow and arrows, or harpoon. Despite the menacing appearance of the Eskimos in their armada Frobisher felt his hopes rise. He was a fighter and could hold his own in combat. The reappearance of the Eskimos gave him a chance to get back his small boat and, possibly, its crew.

Quickly he prepared the *Gabriel* for defence. All chainways and shrouds were covered with canvas, as were all openings where the Eskimos might have been able to climb on board. He mounted the cannon in the waist and trained it on the approaching fleet. Thus began the first, and by far the strangest, naval encounter ever to take place in Canadian Arctic waters. Just how hostile the Eskimos really were will never be known, but to Frobisher, alone with only thirteen men, in a strange land hundreds of miles from home, they were the enemy.

The Eskimo flotilla stopped all movement; the boats floated quietly on the smooth sea. There was no sound as each side looked the other over. Slowly one of the Eskimo hunters began to manoeuvre his kayak towards the *Gabriel*. Frobisher thought it was the same man who had agreed to guide the ship to the west. The Eskimo paddled in close making signs of friendship as he came. Frobisher ordered his men to move back, to lower their arms while he took up position in the waist of the ship by the rail. By signs he bade the Eskimo to come on board.

But the man was wary and held off. Frobisher held out small gifts. The man was interested but wouldn't come close. Frobisher held out a small bell and set it to tinkling. The Eskimo sat quietly, listening. Suddenly Frobisher threw the bell across the water. It landed short of the kayak and the soft sound was cut off sharply as the bell hit the water and sank from sight. The Eskimo was disturbed. He paddled in circles. Frobisher immediately held out another bell and began to shake it. The Eskimo paddled in close and reached out. Quick as a flash Frobisher dropped the bell and grasped the outstretched hand. A quick pull and the man and his kayak were alongside. Reaching down with his free hand Frobisher grasped the man by the shoulders and, with one heave, lifted the Eskimo hunter, kayak and all, into the waist of the ship. The crew rushed in. There was a short struggle during which the man bit off the tip of his tongue, but he was quickly subdued. While he sat morosely on the deck of the *Gabriel*, the other Eskimos fled. In a few minutes they had disappeared around a distant point of land.

Frobisher treated his captive kindly, endeavouring to get him to effect a return of the missing men and the boat, and to guide the *Gabriel* to the west. But the hunter remained surly and unresponsive. For three days Frobisher remained at anchor in the bay hoping for a return of the Eskimos so that he could bargain with them. But not a sign of them did he see; all around the *Gabriel* land and sea remained empty and quiet.

Martin Frobisher realized that he would have to turn back, to accept the disappointment. The season was late, the *Gabriel* was in bad shape, he had lost his only ship's boat and five of his men, and the remaining crew members were beginning to feel the effects of their long and arduous trip. Yet he was far from being discouraged. Vowing to return again the following year, he gave the order to weigh anchor and set sail for England.

Who Was Martin Frobisher?

Who was this man, Martin Frobisher, to whom the discovery of a Northwest Passage to Asia was "the only thing of the world left undone whereby a notable mind might be made famous and fortunate"?[1]

Frobisher was born at Doncaster, Yorkshire, in the year 1540, when King Henry VIII was in the last years of his tempestuous reign as the Merrie Monarch of England. Although brought up in London by his uncle, Sir John York, Frobisher never lost the great love of the sea that is typical of men from the west of England. At the home of his uncle, who was Master of the Mint and a prominent London merchant, Frobisher grew up in a household where conversation was dominated by stories of intrigue at the Royal Court, and by exciting tales of ships' captains just back from profitable trading trips across distant seas.

By the time he was fifteen Frobisher was a seaman before the mast; not an unusual feat in his day when young people grew up quickly and didn't live very long. In fact, Frobisher's first voyage under sail came near to being his last. Off the Guinea coast of Africa a fever killed most of the crew. Frobisher barely escaped with his life. He must have taken this to be a good omen for he remained a seaman and ship's captain to the end of his days. His ships

[1] Sir John Barrow, *Chronological History of Voyages into the Arctic Regions* (London: J. Murray, 1818).

carried coal to Newcastle, silks from the Levant, spices from the African coast.

Whenever trading was slow, Frobisher found profit and excitement raiding and plundering Spanish or Portuguese vessels. For, among his other accomplishments, Martin Frobisher was a pirate. Of course most people in sixteenth-century England didn't think of him as a pirate, even though he was once arrested and imprisoned (but never tried) on a charge of piracy on the high seas. No indeed; in England, Frobisher was a famous figure, a ship's captain, friend of wealthy London merchants, a person highly regarded by Queen Elizabeth. In almost all his ventures he seemed to have some kind of backing from the Queen.

Two of his contemporaries were John Hawkins and Francis Drake. Like Frobisher, Hawkins and Drake were pirates. Hawkins stole Negro slaves from Portuguese ships off Africa and then sold them in the Spanish colonies in the Americas. Drake looted Spanish galleons of their gold as they transported the wealth of South and Central America to their homeland. To the English, Hawkins, Frobisher and Drake were gallant sea dogs. To the Spanish and Portuguese they were pirates. The Spanish called Drake "El Draco," the Dragon. What they called Frobisher is not known but his name was well-known to Spanish nobles and merchants who cursed him as much as they did Hawkins and Drake.

What aroused in Martin Frobisher the desire to discover a Northwest Passage to Asia?

Frobisher lived in a tumultuous age, and he was a true son of his times. In the mid-sixteenth century, Ivan the Terrible ruled Russia. Mongols under Akbar held sway over India. The Ming Dynasty flourished in China. Spain ruled the Atlantic and systematically looted the former Aztec, Maya and Inca empires of their gold. In northern North America French fishermen traded European goods for furs from the Indians at Tadoussac, but Champlain had yet to plant his little colony on the St. Lawrence at Quebec. Mariners were rediscovering the fact that the world was round, although none knew how far around it went. They had no inkling of the extent or outline of northern North America.

In the sixteenth century, wealth and glory awaited the man who could sail, or finance, a ship full of trade goods to the Levant, to the Guinea coast of Africa, to the ports on the Baltic Sea. From Russia ships of the Muscovy Company brought ivory and fine furs. From Baghdad and Damascus the Levant Company brought silks and jewels, and spices by the ton. Merchant ships from England were beginning to sail all the way to India. Others would soon strike out across the north Atlantic, to tap the great forest of fur that lay waiting in the sub-Arctic region of North America.

Much as we might prefer to think of more noble motives for the early geographic discoveries by European explorers, it was simple greed that first set the eyes of western man towards the far corners of the world. Wealth, and the power and glory it produced, were what men from Europe sought as they sailed their tiny vessels off into the unknown, or as they sat in their palaces and counting houses awaiting the return of the ships their money had bought and provisioned. They didn't want to find new land; they sought old lands from whence came the silks, jewels, dyes, rare herbs and spices that Europe had long imported over the ship and caravan routes through the Near East and Mediterranean lands.

Pepper was one mainstay of this trade. Beef and mutton were staple foods in Middle Age Europe and England. In fact they were almost the only food, for potatoes and vegetables as we know them today were unknown as were coffee, tea and cocoa. People ate meat. The rich drank wine; the poor a small beer or water. But large herds of sheep and cattle couldn't be pastured during the winter months and most were slaughtered in the autumn and the meat dried or salted. Pepper, and other spices, made this meat palatable during the long months of winter, and all Europeans came to depend on its use.

Pepper came to Europe from the Orient: by ship across the Indian Ocean and the Mediterranean Sea; by land along the great caravan routes through the fabled lands of the Middle East. Transportation costs were high and made higher by the ever-increasing number of middlemen who became engaged in this trade. In thirteenth century Europe, two hundredweight of pepper cost £50 sterling at the Mediterranean port of Marseilles. By the time it reached England the price had increased to 80 pounds.

As consumption increased with population growth, so did the cost of transportation continue to rise. By the end of the fifteenth century, western Europe and England were consuming immense quantities of meat, most of which they flavoured heavily with pepper and other Oriental spices. In addition, many spices were used liberally in medicines for human ailments (the hotter the medicine, the more effective it was supposed to be). For all Europe the need for direct access to the sources of supply became an economic necessity which was made even more acute when, in 1453, the Turks captured Constantinople and thus cut off the land transport routes between Europe and the East. In 1517 the Turks conquered Egypt and controlled the Mediterranean sea lanes. The way to Asia by the East was closed to western Europe but the need for silks and spices remained as strong as ever.

Portugal sent ships south to explore and develop a trade route around the southern tip of Africa. Spanish vessels crossed the Atlantic to Central and South America, then passed through the Strait of Magellan to the Pacific. France, Germany, Holland and England, cut off from these sea routes by the papal edict of 1494 which divided all new land in the western hemisphere between Spain and Portugal, sent ships west, northwest and north, reaching out over the roof of the world in an attempt to find a direct water route to the rich lands of Cathay.

The French explorer, Cartier, found the water gateway of the St. Lawrence River, which diverted the French from the task of exploration to the northwest. Cabot and Corte-Real sailed northwest but found no sign of a passage. Germany and Holland soon lost interest, following the meagre results attained from the early voyages. In the late sixteenth century the need for a Northwest Passage lessened. In 1571 the naval battle of Lepanto broke the Ottoman hold on the Mediterranean Sea routes. Most European merchants saw little need to divert money and ships from the well-established and profitable trade routes towards a costly and uncertain search for a sea route through northern waters.

It was mainly in England, the island nation facing out onto the north Atlantic, that the idea of a Northwest Passage to Asia refused to die. One of its strongest proponents was the Elizabethan sea dog Martin Frobisher.

All Is Not Gold . . .

F robisher returned to England, from his first trip to Baffin Island, on October 1, 1576. He was given a joyous welcome. The *Michael* had reported the *Gabriel* lost with all hands and it seemed as if Frobisher and his men had returned from the dead. Londoners were fascinated by the Eskimo hunter and his strange little craft. Unfortunately he caught a cold on the return trip and died about a month after reaching England.

Except for a lucky accident Frobisher's hopes for a second voyage would have died that autumn as well. For, although he was in great demand to tell the story of his adventures in the strange land he had discovered, Frobisher had little to show as a result of the expedition but the Eskimo hunter and a shining black rock which he gave to Michael Lok, his principal supporter, as "the fyrst thynge that he founde in the newland."[1]

Lok's wife wasn't particularly pleased with such a meagre return on the more than £800 that Lok had put up as his share of the expenses of the expedition. She promptly threw the rock into the fire, where ". . . at lengthe it being taken forth, and quenched in a little vinegre, it glistened with a bright Masquesset of goldc."[2]

[1] Richard Hakluyt, *The Principall Navigations . . .* , p. 283.
[2] *Ibid.*, p. 283.

Gold! The search for a Northwest Passage was all but forgotten. Lok took the stone to a number of assayers all of whom pronounced it worthless. But Lok was persistent in his belief that the stone contained gold. Eventually he took it to an Italian assayer, John Baptista Agnello, who returned to Lok a small sample of gold he said he had found in the stone. Immediately Lok took Agnello's findings to Queen Elizabeth with a request for funds towards an expedition to mine the ore. Elizabeth, always canny, had additional tests made by other assayers, all of whom reported the stone to be without value.

But Lok managed to find a second assayer, a friend of Agnello, who also reported gold in the stone. This was enough to convince most people of its worth, even the Queen. Lok had little difficulty getting commercial and Royal backing for the formation of a new company, "The Companye of Kathai,"[3] to send ships and men to Baffin Island to mine for ore. Michael Lok was appointed Governor of the company for life, and Frobisher was made "High Admyrall of all Seas and Waters, Countryes and Places of New Discovery."[4] By a stroke of Queen Elizabeth's pen Martin Frobisher had become "Lord of Southern Baffin Island."[5]

Although Frobisher was granted permission to make a limited search into his "strait" if circumstances permitted, the main objective of the expedition was to mine for gold. With three ships he sailed west across the Atlantic and reached the entrance to his strait without mishap, which speaks well of his navigation. In the waterway Frobisher again met Eskimos and the first meeting was friendly. Then he tried to capture a hostage or two in order to barter for his missing men from the year before, if they should still be alive. He captured one Eskimo hunter but only after a confused struggle in which Frobisher received an arrow wound in the buttocks for his trouble.

[3] Richard Hakluyt, *The Principall Navigations.* . . .
[4] *Ibid.*
[5] *Ibid.*

At a place called Bloody Point he and his men fought a pitched battle with the Eskimos, killing five or six hunters and capturing two women, one very old and the other young with a child. The old woman was so ugly that she was suspected of being a witch. Frobisher promptly let her go. The young one was taken on board where she proved to be a faithful companion for the hunter captured previously. From his captives Frobisher tried to get information about his missing men but without success. He did find scraps of clothing in abandoned Eskimo houses and he thought the Eskimos indicated to him that the men still lived, but he saw no other sign of them. From a small island his men took about 200 tons of ore that an assayer friend of Agnello's, who was with the expedition, said was rich with gold. With the 200 tons of ore and his Eskimo prisoners, Frobisher took his ships back to England.

Once again he was greeted with great joy by the Queen, and by the Cathay Company stockholders. The Queen was delighted with the Eskimo man and woman. She granted the man permission to hunt the Royal swans from his kayak. Unfortunately, both died not long after reaching England. An autopsy was performed on the body of the man and the report of it still exists as a State Paper ("Report of the Sicknesse and Death of the Man at Bristol which Capt. Furbisher brought from the Northwst.").[6] He died of a lung condition, complicated by two broken ribs which had failed to heal properly.

Tests on the ore brought back, again conducted by Agnello, indicated that a handsome profit could be made on the gold it contained. Additional tests were conducted by a group of experts who stated that the ore ". . . had appearance, and made show of great profit and wealth."[7] Queen Elizabeth was overwhelmed by the prospect of such riches; she received Frobisher at Court and awarded him a bonus of £100. There was no difficulty in finding additional backers to invest funds in the Cathay

[6] A. Copland, "Eskimo in Captivity," *North*, XIV (March-April, 1967), p. 1.
[7] Richard Hakluyt, *The Principall Navigations . . .* , p. 319.

Company and plans were drawn up to build a mill and smelter on the Thames, to be supplied with ore by a large expedition sent to Baffin Island in the summer of 1578.

The third voyage of Martin Frobisher, like the second, achieved nothing in the way of discovery of a Northwest Passage to Asia, but it ranks as one of the most ambitious Arctic expeditions ever undertaken in the Canadian north. No other expedition before or since has come close to matching it in sheer size and scope. It chalked up more firsts than any other voyage for years to come. One or two of the records it set stand unbeaten to this day.

Its main objective was to bring back at least 2,000 tons of ore. In addition, it was planned to establish a small colony of about 120 men who would remain at the mine site through the following winter in order to continue work at the mine as soon as weather conditions permitted in the spring, and to study the climate and other physical aspects of the new land. It was felt that such a colony could support itself by profits from the mining venture, and that it would provide an advanced base from which ships could push through "Frobisher's Streights" to the Pacific. Carpenters, miners, soldiers were recruited. Tons of supplies were purchased. A wooden fort was built in sections which could be assembled quickly at the mine site to provide a comfortable dwelling for the wintering party. This marked the first time that a prefabricated building was to be used on an Arctic expedition. An Anglican clergyman by the name of Wolfal accompanied the expedition hoping to establish the first mission to the Eskimos in North America.

Although many private backers had invested funds in the Cathay Company, the expedition to Baffin Island was organized under the direct supervision of the Queen and her ministers. A fleet of fifteen vessels was assembled, the largest ever to sail to the Canadian Arctic, a record that has yet to be bettered. The ships ranged in size from the tiny *Moon*, smaller than either the *Gabriel* or the *Michael*, up to the *Thomas Allen*, a 400-tonner under the command of the Vice-Admiral of the fleet, Captain Yorke. Frobisher's flagship was the *Aid*, a vessel of about 200 tons. Many of the veterans of the earlier voyages sailed with the fleet; Edward Fenton was chosen as the person to remain behind as Governor of the colony, George Beste was to chronicle the story of the expedition, Christopher Hall was the Chief Pilot, Charles Jackman was named pilot for "any discoverie to ye westwarde."[8]

On his previous two voyages Frobisher had had about an equal amount of good and bad fortune with wind, ice and weather. On the third trip luck ran out completely. Leading his fleet across the Atlantic he found Queen Elizabeth's Foreland without difficulty, but there his troubles began. The year 1578 was very bad for ice in Davis Strait and "Frobisher's Streightes" was similarly clogged. For days the ships struggled to get ahead. In frequent storms they became separated from each other time and time again. One ship, the small bark containing some of the building sections for the house, sank after colliding with an iceberg. Another ship gave up the struggle and returned to England.

It was the 7th of July before Frobisher was able to work his fleet of thirteen ships into what he thought was his strait. Westward he sailed for nearly 200 miles before the surprisingly swift currents and rushing tides convinced him he was in the wrong channel. He turned about and sailed back east, calling the new water "Mistaken Straits." We know it as Hudson Strait and if Frobisher had kept going his name might well be on the maps of today to mark the great inland sea we call Hudson Bay. In a masterful display of seamanship and leadership, Frobisher successfully led his flotilla north through dangerous fields of heavy, moving ice in the unexplored channel between Resolution Island and Baffin Island. On July 31st the ships came to anchor in Countess of Warwick's Sound and began to take on their loads of ore.

[8] Richard Hakluyt, *The Principall Navigations.* . . .

Frobisher was unable to establish the colony. The loss of the building sections on the sunken ship made it impossible to construct the house as planned. Some of the men volunteered to remain behind for the winter if the carpenters could build a smaller house with the remaining materials but, in the time available, this could not be done. This probably saved the lives of the sixty or so volunteers for there is little doubt that most would have perished in the ensuing winter as a result of the ravages of scurvy. The clergyman had to abandon his idea of a mission to the Eskimos but he did celebrate the first Anglican Communion service ever held on Canadian soil. The men built a house of lime and stone into which they put toys and other articles, including an oven complete with freshly baked bread, to show the Eskimos their peaceful intent.

On August 30th, with holds full of ore, the fleet sailed away from Baffin Island. Ice and storm threatened them with disaster in Frobisher Bay. The ships were separated by storms in the north Atlantic, but, one by one, they struggled back to England. By October 1st all had returned safely home.

It was not a joyful return. In their absence the mining bubble had burst. The first mining operation in Canada became the first to go bankrupt. Somehow sanity had prevailed and the ore from Baffin Island had been pronounced worthless. It contained not gold, but iron pyrite—fool's gold. Much of the ore was later used as road-building material in southern England. The remainder was dumped into the harbour at Bristol where, nearly 400 years later, it would damage a dredge digging on the harbour bottom. The Cathay Company was bankrupt. Michael Lok was tossed into debtor's prison. There seems to be no record of the feelings of the Queen.

Martin Frobisher found no passage to Asia but he believed to the end of his days that the channel he discovered was a strait leading to open water, across which ships could sail direct to Cathay. He was not proven wrong for nearly 300 years, until, in 1862, the American explorer Charles Francis Hall journeyed to the bottom of Frobisher Bay and found it to be landlocked. On the way he discovered relics of mining and settlement that Frobisher's men had left behind, and he heard from the Eskimos, for the first time, their story of the great ships that had come to their land long, long ago.

Many, many years ago, long before the time of my grandfather's grandfather, white men came to our land. They came in summer, in great ships with wings of white. For three summers the ships came, first two ships, then three, then many ships. After that our people saw them no more.

The white men killed five of our people and they took two more with them when they departed our land. These two, a man and a woman, were never seen again. But our people captured five of the white men who came ashore in one of their boats. These men lived among our people. We did not harm them, but they desired to return to their land across the sea. After the second winter they dug up wood left behind by their friends. They built a ship with a tall mast. In the ship the five white men tried to sail away to the east. But they set off too early in the season, while the bay was still full of drifting ice. They froze their hands and their feet and had to return. They all died in our land.

All these things happened long, long ago. But we know about them because our fathers told us, just as their fathers told them. And, on Kodlunarn Island, you can still see the marks the white men made on our land long, long ago.[9]

Martin Frobisher never returned to Canada to follow up his belief in his strait. Resourceful as ever, he was quick to recover his fortunes. He had been a practising pirate before he set off to find a sea route over the roof of the world, and pirates in any age are hard to keep down. In 1583 he joined the Queen's Navy and

---

[9] This account was composed by the author, based on material in C. F. Hall's book, *Life with the Esquimaux* (Edmonton: M. G. Hurtig Ltd.), and supplemented by personal talks with Eskimo hunters at Frobisher Bay.

quickly rose in favour and rank until he commanded one of the largest ships of the line. With his old friends Hawkins and Drake he took part in the great naval action that saw the defeat of the Spanish Armada in 1588, for which service he was knighted by his Queen.

In 1594, at the age of fifty-four, Frobisher was mortally wounded while fighting the Spaniards in front of Brest. He died in Plymouth and was buried in London. Today, on Baffin Island, the modern town of Frobisher Bay dominates the landscape at the western end of his "streightes," honouring a brave and resolute man. He was one of those few who travel far because they can see far, when they are filled with the unquenchable spirit of adventure, and the insatiable desire to know.

Journey to Hudson Bay

Winnipeg International Airport. Quiet in the pre-dawn darkness of a bitterly cold February day. Out of the northwest the wind blows, boisterously, bringing to southern Canada the feel of concentrated cold of the Arctic tundra far away to the north. Muffled men shuffle about the ground carts, swinging their arms to keep warm as the line of hurrying passengers scurries to the waiting plane. A stewardess in stretch slacks greets them as they enter the warmth of the plane's interior. The door swings shut. TransAir Flight No. 131 taxies out for takeoff. Destination: the northern town of Churchill on Hudson Bay.

The takeoff is smooth. Slowly the plane banks until it is climbing due north. Beneath the silver wings the stone walls of Lower Fort Garry catch the first red rays of the rising sun, just as they must have done on other February mornings 100 years ago when Sir George Simpson ruled his western empire of fur from this lovely fort on the banks of the Red River. The trees in the park at Seven Oaks stand out against white snow, on the ground once stained red with the blood of the murdered Scots colonists sent to this lonely land by Lord Selkirk to populate his kingdom of Assiniboia.

Northward the plane flies, 30,000 feet over Lake Winnipeg, high above the lakes and rivers that once formed the main highway into western Canada from Hudson Bay. Today you travel this route at 550 miles per hour. In 1819 John Franklin averaged ten to twelve miles per day. This is the land of the fur trade, of Kelsey and Henday, McDonell and Simpson, Mackintosh and McLeod. Once it was called Rupert's Land after the first Governor of the famous company known as "The Governor and Company of Adventurers Trading into Hudson Bay." It is still called Rupert's Land by the Anglican Church in Canada.

Four hours after departure from Winnipeg the plane begins to let down. Snow-covered lake and bush give way to flat land scattered with patches of stubby trees through which, straight as an arrow pointing north, runs the thin ribbon of rail connecting Winnipeg to Manitoba's only seaport. Far off to the north a dark cloud hangs low on the horizon—steam rising from the open waters along the floe edge of Hudson Bay. The plane banks sharply and the grain elevator and docks of Churchill come into view. The entire town is a mere speck in the immensity of snow-covered land and sea that stretches away for hundreds of miles in every direction.

Churchill is Canada's main Arctic seaport, the only one with proper harbour facilities that are connected to the south by rail. Unlike Frobisher Bay on Baffin Island, 1,000 miles to the northeast, Churchill presents no picture of bustling modernity. Here there are no large apartment buildings, no rows of new houses, no humming activity of a growing town. Churchill in midwinter resembles any other small prairie town: a wide, snow-covered main street flanked by small stores and even smaller houses, an empty square facing an old-fashioned railway station, the whole scene dominated by the immense bulk of the huge, white grain elevator.[1]

But, like Frobisher Bay, history at Churchill is never far away. Jump into an oversnow vehicle, preferably one with an

[1] This picture will soon change, due to a new ten million dollar development program for the Churchill area.

enclosed cab and a good heater, for the temperature stands at thirty below and the ten knot wind out of the northwest sends the wind chill factor down to fifty-three below. Drive down the road and over the railway tracks to the riverbank beside the grain elevator. Be careful getting down onto the ice of the river —it is broken and hummocked by the action of the Hudson Bay tides in the river mouth, and there are pools of deep slush in the cracks. Then, full speed across the smooth middle ice to the flat point of land on the far side. Through the jumbled ice again, and up a long, gentle slope. Stop beside a stone wall almost buried in a deep drift of unbroken snow.

To the south you can still see the grain elevator looming starkly against the pale blue sky. You can see the train shunting freight cars through the ground drift that swirls along the line of docks. Above the whistle of the wind you hear the train hoot, the cars clank—sounds of a twentieth-century prairie town. But turn about and face into the northwest wind. Instantly, almost as if by magic, you have stepped backward 200 years in time.

Fifty feet away the immense stone walls of an ancient fur-trade fort lie almost buried in the deep, hard-packed drifts. Walk up the sloping snowbank towards the main entrance to the fort and read the inscription carved in the stone: "Fort Prince of Wales, 1771." Scramble down into the partially snow-filled entrance tunnel, and walk through to the inner courtyard beyond. The footing is difficult on the slippery, hard-packed snow. Climb the steps to the wide gallery where blades of brown grass poke upward to bob in the bitter wind. You are startled by a sudden swoosh of flapping wings as a flock of ptarmigan leaps into full flight to disappear almost immediately over the far wall. Stand beside one of the rusting iron cannons, already old when it was installed in its embrasure more than 200 years ago, and look out across the wind-swept, ice-covered surface of Hudson Bay.

Hudson Bay—Arctic hunters knew of it thousands of years ago. For centuries Indians of the northern bush hunted whales and bears along its southern shore. Long before Cartier came to the St. Lawrence, Norse from Greenland may have passed this way. Martin Frobisher almost became the first European to sail its waters, but it was thirty years after Frobisher turned back in his "Mistaken Straits" before another European, again an Englishman, sailed his ship across the north Atlantic, through Hudson Strait and out onto the wide expanse of this immense inland sea.

Like Frobisher before him, Henry Hudson sought a Northwest Passage to Cathay. Before coming to Arctic Canada he had sailed for the Dutch to the north of Asia, and to the east coast of America where he discovered the river that now bears his name. It was in the year 1610 that he came to northern North America, in his small ship *Discovery*, to successfully navigate his strait and discover his bay. He sailed south in the bay, hoping to find a way to Asia. Instead he was trapped into spending a winter on the east shore of James Bay. During the winter serious dissension spread amongst his officers and crew, and, by petty dealing, Hudson lost the respect of many of his men.

It was mid-June of 1611 before the men could get the ship free from the ice and set off for home. By this time many had had their fill of Hudson. A mutiny took place. Henry Hudson and seven others were set adrift in a small boat in lower Hudson Bay, never to be seen again.[2] The mutineers sailed the ship north to Cape Digges where five of the ringleaders were killed in a fight with Eskimos. The remainder, under Robert Bylot, former mate, sailed the ship back to England where all managed to escape punishment for their crime.

In 1612 Thomas Button, with Robert Bylot as pilot, sailed to Hudson Bay and charted sections of the west coast, but he found no sign of a passage to the West. He didn't bother to look for Henry Hudson. In 1615 Bylot returned again, in Hudson's old

---

[2] There is an Eskimo legend that tells of a small boat containing the bodies of an old man with a bushy beard and a young boy being washed ashore on the east coast of Hudson Bay. Henry Hudson and his son?

ship *Discovery*, but he got no farther than Southampton Island before heavy ice stopped his ship and forced him to return to England. In 1631 Luke Foxe and Thomas James both headed sailing expeditions to Hudson Bay, charting sections of the west coast, but, like the others before them, they found no sign of a Northwest Passage to Asia. With this, English interest in a possible sea route across Arctic America went into decline.

There had been another expedition to Hudson Bay in the year 1619, sent out by the Danish King and commanded by Jens Munck. In two ships, the *Unicorn* and the *Lamprey*, Munck sailed to the west coast of Hudson Bay not far from the mouth of Chesterfield Inlet. From there he turned south and, like Hudson, was trapped into spending a winter in the Canadian north. On the west bank of the Churchill River, about five miles from the present site of Fort Prince of Wales, Munck and his men hauled out their boats and built a small fort of wood.

The winter was one of unrelieved horror. Until Christmas the men lived fairly well, but then scurvy began to take its dreadful toll. By the time the ice on the river went out in July, only Munck and two other men were left to sail the *Lamprey* back to Denmark. Sixty men died of starvation and cold, their frozen bodies left behind in the grim land they had found. Men had been lost on expeditions to Canada's Arctic in the years before 1610 but it was with the abandonment of Hudson and the tragedy of Munck that the terrible toll of death and disaster in Arctic Canada really began. Before it was over hundreds were to lie in unknown and unmarked graves across the top of North America.

That's right. Shiver a little as you stand on the shore of this frozen sea. The wind out of the northwest is bitterly cold. Colder still is the thought of the brave men who died not far from here in those days of long ago.

Turn now and look down into the main courtyard of Fort Prince of Wales, silent except for the whistle of the wind, empty but for its huge drifts of snow. Once men lived and worked inside these stone walls, young men from England and Scotland come to trade with the Indians for their furs. They had food and shelter, and a measure of comfort. But, in the mid-eighteenth century, life inside Fort Prince of Wales was austere.

> In the month of January the cold began to be extremely intense. The head of my bed rested against one of the outside walls of the fort and, notwithstanding they were of stone and near three feet thick, lined with inch boards, my bedding was frozen to the boards every morning. It was almost impossible to sleep an hour together without being awakened by the cracking of the beams which were rent by the prodigious power of the frost. It was easy to mistake them for guns on the top of the house.[3]

Who were these men who lived on the shores of Hudson Bay over 200 years ago? Walk along the shore of the river, upstream from the fort, until you come to a small cove where smooth, ice-scoured rocks slope gently down to the broken ice. Scrape away the thin cover of snow from the rock and there before you, stencilled in stone, is the record of their passing. The names and dates were carved 200 years ago as men wiled away their leisure hours in this lonely land, far from home.

> George Holt—1771 [George Holt was master of the Hudson's Bay Company sloop *Churchill*]
> Richard Camm—1747 [Richard Camm was a seaman aboard the Company ship *Seahorse*]
> Robert Smith—1776 [Robert Smith was a shipwright at Fort Prince of Wales]
> William Davisson—1747 [William Davisson's occupation is unknown, but his wages were £27 per year]
> John Kelley—1764 [John Kelley was a seaman, and the

[3] This is a condensed version of a passage by Oliver Fuller in "The Mariners at Sloop Cove," *The Beaver* (Summer, 1963).

drawing beside his name suggests that he may have been hanged for stealing a goose][4]

If you search carefully, digging down through the deeper snow, you will soon come to another name carved in the rock.

S' Hearne—July VI, 1767

Look at this name carefully, then turn and look west over the scrub bush that extends away from you as far as your eyes can see, bush that flows northwest from here for over 1,000 miles before it peters out into a narrow strip of tundra on the shores of the northern sea. Between you and the mouth of the Copper-mine River there is nothing but mile after lonely mile of stunt-ed, sub-Arctic forest—"Land of the Little Sticks." In the mid-eighteenth century this was a completely unknown country. No European had penetrated more than a few miles inland from Fort Prince of Wales. None knew how far land extended to the west. None knew where the north coast of America might lie. Until, in the year 1771, the young Englishman who carved his name in the rocks at your feet, Samuel Hearne, walked over-land, searching for a river where copper was reputed to lie in sight on the ground, not far from the shores of a frozen northern sea.

[4] Reproductions of the actual signatures on the rocks appear in the *Beaver* article just cited (Summer, 1963). See pages 46-52.

Who Was Samuel Hearne?

When Samuel Hearne was born in London, in the year 1745, Britain was at war with France and Spain, fighting in Europe, in India, and in North America. A year later the Highlanders of Scotland marched into England, in support of the invasion attempt by Bonnie Prince Charles, only to meet defeat on Culloden field. In 1745, the British force of American colonists from New England captured the great French fort at Louisbourg. It was also the year that marked the beginning of the end for British rule of the Thirteen Colonies in America, and for French rule over her American empire on the St. Lawrence.

For seventy-five years the Hudson's Bay Company had been trading for fur through the Hudson Strait gateway into Canada, its ships following the path opened up by the voyages of Frobisher, Hudson, Foxe and James. The open water of Hudson Strait had not led men to the riches of Cathay, but it had opened up a different kind of Eldorado—the great forest of fur of the sub-Arctic Canadian bush. From their small forts, built at the mouths of the rivers flowing north into Hudson and James bays, the Hudson's Bay Company traded guns, axes and blankets for beaver, martin and fox. They had opposition: the French claimed this land as theirs, and English fought

French for control of the northern fur trade. Forts were sacked and burned, furs and traders captured, ships were seized or sunk.

In one classic naval battle on Hudson Bay off the mouth of the Nelson River in 1697, the French under M. d'Iberville, fighting from the *Pelican*, engaged three English ships—the *Dering* and the *Hudson's Bay*, two lightly armed merchantmen, and the *Hampshire*, a British naval vessel of fifty-six guns. In the fight, the *Dering* and the *Hudson's Bay* fled after the first encounter. The *Hampshire* sank after taking a broadside from the *Pelican*, and then running hard onto a hidden shoal. This was a far cry from Martin Frobisher's naval encounter with the Eskimos 120 years before.

The Hudson's Bay Company had first established a wooden fort at the mouth of the Churchill River in the year 1717, on the site where Munck's men had died so horribly nearly 100 years before. This fort burned to the ground during construction and, in 1732, building was started on Fort Prince of Wales, which was to become the northern trading headquarters and military bastion of the Company on Hudson Bay. The immense stone fort took nearly forty years to build, but, for all its massive walls and strategic position guarding the mouth of the Churchill River, it proved to be merely a showpiece. Its cannon were obsolete, it had no naval support, and it was undermanned by a small band of Company personnel. In 1782 it fell to the French under La Pérouse, without a shot being fired in its defence.

Samuel Hearne came to Fort Prince of Wales in the year 1766. He was only twenty-one years of age but already a veteran of six years' active service with the British Navy. He had joined the Navy at the age of twelve as Captain's servant to Samuel Hood, later Admiral Lord Hood. For six years Hearne served with the Navy at sea in wartime. He was on board the frigate *Vestal* in February of 1759 when this vessel engaged in a ship-to-ship battle with the French frigate *Bellona*. He took part in the great bombardment at Le Havre. Later his ship fought in the Mediterranean where he sailed as far as Turkey and saw Gibraltar under siege by the Spanish.

This was a tough apprenticeship for a young boy just entering his teens. In the mid-eighteenth century, life on board vessels of the British Navy was grim. On the *Vestal*, 210 men were crammed into a ship only 175 feet overall. Constantly at sea, in good weather and bad, living in dark, filthy between-deck accommodation that swarmed with rats, life was anything but pleasant. And the food! The endless monotony of salted meat, often bad, and ship's biscuit, often hard as iron. In the biscuits lived dozens of weevils, so many that it was possible to swallow fifteen to twenty in one bite. Each meal began with a ritual tattoo—seamen banging their biscuits on the table to shake loose the weevils.

> A ship is worse than a gaol. There is, in gaol, better air, better company, better convenience of every kind; and a ship has the additional disadvantage of being in danger.[1]

Such was Samuel Hearne's life between the ages of twelve and eighteen. By the time he was discharged from the Navy in 1763, he was as tough as nails.

When he was twenty-one, Hearne joined the Hudson's Bay Company as a seaman and was sent to Fort Prince of Wales on Hudson Bay. For two summers he sailed north on the Company sloop to catch whales in the waters off Marble Island, and to trade with groups of Eskimos living on the west coast of the bay. He enjoyed his life in the Canadian north. In 1768 he requested the Company to give him command of one of its ships on the bay. But, quite unknown to Hearne, his employers had other plans for his future.

Although interest in a Northwest Passage remained at a low ebb in the years following Foxe's and James' voyages, the Hudson's Bay Company had conducted searches for a possible

---

[1] Samuel Johnson

passage to the west of Hudson Bay. James Knight, who must hold the record for being the oldest explorer ever to sail in Arctic waters (he was nearly eighty when he sailed north from Churchill in 1719), disappeared on a voyage in search of a route to the west. Fifty years were to pass before it was established that he and all his men starved to death on Marble Island off the west coast of the bay. Fifty more names added to the growing toll of dead and missing in Arctic Canada.

In 1741 Captain Middleton explored the west coast as far north as Repulse Bay, but his ship was stopped from entering Frozen Strait by heavy ice. In 1746 Captain Moore found Wager Inlet to be an enclosed bay. In 1762 Captain Christopher established that Chesterfield Inlet led only to Baker Lake. There seemed to be no possible Northwest Passage waterway west from Hudson Bay.

But myth died hard in the eighteenth century, and the myth of a strait that led from the west coast of North America (in the vicinity of present day Vancouver), northeast to ice-free water somewhere in the north Atlantic, had been firmly rooted in men's minds for over 200 years. The Hudson's Bay Company was under constant pressure in London to search for such a strait. Many opponents of the Company's monopoly charter, particularly one Arthur Dobbs, claimed that under the terms of the charter the Company was legally bound to press the search for a Northwest Passage with more vigour than it had shown. Thus, when Moses Norton, the Governor for the Company at Fort Prince of Wales, appeared before the Committee in London in 1769 with a plan to send a small overland expedition to the northwest from the fort, to search for a passage and to establish the truth about copper mines reported to lie beside the frozen northern sea, his plan was quickly accepted. The man chosen to lead the expedition was Samuel Hearne.

The Hudson's Bay Company rarely seemed able to attract into its employ a good supply of men with vision and daring, but it did have the happy faculty of coming up with just the right man, at just the right time, during certain key phases of its long history. Such was the case with Samuel Hearne. Although Hearne was a seaman he had undertaken long trips in winter between Company posts on the bay and he was familiar with all aspects of wood travel. With his background in the Navy, and as a result of his winter trips in Canada, he was tough and persevering, inured to almost any hardship. Even among the Indians he was renowned as being "fleet of foot on snowshoes."[2] He hadn't given much thought towards exploration for a Northwest Passage but, when he "was pitched as the proper person to conduct the expedition"[3] Hearne was ready to go. On the 6th of November, 1769, to a salute from six of the cannon, he led his party through the gate of Fort Prince of Wales and started out on his first long walk across northern Canada in search of the northern sea.

The trip nearly ended in disaster. Planning of the expedition, and the choice of the Indians to go along as guides and hunters, was the responsibility of the Governor, Moses Norton. Norton was a half-breed, son of a former governor of the fort, educated in England for nine years during his youth. Hearne described him as a man who:

> . . . kept for his own use five or six of the finest Indian girls. . . .
> his apartments were not only convenient but elegant and
> always crowded with favourite Indians. . . . always kept a box
> of poison to administer to those who refused him their wives
> or daughters. . . . to his own friends and country he was so
> partial, that he set more value on, and shewed more respect
> to one of their favourite dogs, than he ever did to his first
> officer.[4]

Norton showed himself to be quite incapable of making satisfactory arrangements for the conduct of the expedition.

[2] Samuel Hearne, *A Journey to the Northern Ocean*, Ed. by Richard Glover (Toronto: The Macmillan Company of Canada, 1958), p. 163.
[3] *Ibid.*, p. xiii.
[4] *Ibid.*, p. 39.

Hearne travelled with two Company servants from the fort, two Cree Indians from Churchill, and a party of Chipewyan Indian hunters under the leadership of a Captain[5] named Chawchinahaw, who was to be his guide. Chawchinahaw soon disclosed that he had never been to the copper mines and had no idea of the route they should take to reach the northern sea. His Indians hunted little, preferring to eat up the scanty supplies that Hearne had brought from the fort. Within two weeks of leaving Fort Prince of Wales, the explorer had taken all authority for guiding the expedition out of the hands of Chawchinahaw. Hearne set off to lead his small party northwest, while the other Indians, under Chawchinahaw, travelled separately some distance off.

The situation went from bad to worse. Hearne's group got little game because Chawchinahaw's hunters walked out ahead, frightening off any game they did not kill, then refused to share the meat with Hearne and his men. A few of the men deserted, stealing ammunition when they left. On the 24th of November Chawchinahaw and his Chipewyans disappeared completely, declaring they did not know the way to go, and that they had to look after their families. By this time Hearne was about 200 miles northwest of Fort Prince of Wales. His small group had almost no food, he had no idea of the route to follow to the northwest, and the severest winter weather lay ahead. There was nothing to do but turn about and try to get back to the fort. They just made it, barely escaping death by starvation. On December 11th Hearne led his men back through the gate of Fort Prince of Wales "to my own great mortification, and to the no small surprise of the Governor."[6]

Hearne was far from discouraged by his experience. He was used to hardship and shrewd enough to evaluate the lessons

[5] A Captain was an Indian who was recognized by the factors as being a person of importance in his group and through whom all Company business with the group was transacted.

[6] Samuel Hearne, *A Journey* . . . , p. 7.

learned from the venture. He would try again and this time he would take no other Company men with him for he had seen how the Indians had treated with disdain the lower echelon Company employees, once away from the fort. Most important, he had seen how it was next to impossible to direct a northern Indian on such an enterprise when the Indian was disinclined to press on with the task ahead. Unfortunately, his theoretical reasoning did him little good. Again, Moses Norton supervised the organization of the expedition. Again he showed the same lack of understanding as he had shown in planning the first.

With another band of Indians under the leadership of one Conneequeessee, Hearne set off in February 1770. This time there was no salute from the cannon, just three hearty cheers from those remaining behind. Hearne needed far more than cheers for it soon became apparent that Conneequeessee knew even less about the route to follow than had Chawchinahaw. He had never been to the country of the copper mines and he had no idea how far west they would have to travel to reach the frozen northern sea.

For six months, all through the spring and summer of 1770, Hearne found himself wandering in a wide circuit over the tundra between Dubawnt Lake and Hudson Bay while the Indians hunted for caribou. In July he lived for a time in a great camp of some 600 Indians who were living well from the great, northward migrating herds. Finally, on August 11th, he broke his quadrant. It was blown over in a high wind and shattered on a rock. Without it he could not proceed, for it was his only means of establishing latitude in whatever regions he should visit. Once again he was forced to turn back and once again he was deserted and robbed of almost all his possessions by the Indians.

But as he walked back towards Fort Prince of Wales, Hearne's luck began to change. On the way he met the one man in northern Canada who had the knowledge and ability to guide him to the northern sea—a Chipewyan Indian chief named Matonabbee.

Matonabbee listened to Hearne's tales of his travels and troubles, and quickly diagnosed the problems. He offered to guide Hearne to the copper mines on the north coast. He knew where they were for he had been north to the frozen sea. Hearne and Matonabbee became fast friends and remained so for as long as they lived. Together they returned to Fort Prince of Wales with plans for a third trip already made, determined that Moses Norton, despite his great authority as Governor, would have no part in the organization of the third expedition.

By Land to the Northern Ocean

O RDERS and INSTRUCTIONS for Mr. Samuel Hearne, going on his third Expedition to the north of Churchill River, in quest of a North West Passage, Copper Mines, or any other thing that may be servicable to the British Nation in general, or the Hudson's Bay Company in particular; in the year 1770.

Mr. Samuel Hearne.
Sir,

As you have offered your service a third time to go in search of the Copper Mine River, &c., and as Matonabbee, a leading Indian, who has been at these parts, is willing to be your guide, we have accordingly engaged him for that service. . . .

The above Leader, Matonabbee, and a few of his best men, which he has selected for that purpose, are to provide for you, assist you in all things, and conduct you to the Copper Mine River. . . .

As you and your Indian companions are fitted out with everything we think is necessary (or at least as many useful articles as the nature of travelling in these parts will admit of), you are hereby desired to proceed on your journey as soon as possible. . . .

I conclude with my best wishes for your health and

happiness, together with a successful journey, and a quick return in safety. Amen.

[Signed] Moses Norton, Governor.

Dated at Prince of Wales's Fort,
   7th December 1770.[1]

Daylight came late to Fort Prince of Wales in December. It was nine in the morning before the grey light dispelled the last of the deep shadows within the heavy stone walls. The soft yellow light of lanterns threw flickering shadows over the packed snow of the inner compound as Samuel Hearne slipped into his snowshoes and swung his huge pack on his back. He tugged at his deerskin jacket, pulled on his beaded deerskin mitts and took his musket from a friend. With a last look about, he turned and walked out through the entrance tunnel of the fort.

Beyond the walls waited a group of Indians, men, women, and a few children to the number of about twenty. One of the men stepped forward and for a few moments the two stood talking. Matonabbee was tall and muscular, his dark, noble face lined by the cold of many northern winters in the bush. Beside him, Hearne seemed tiny, almost insignificant until you noticed the resolute set to the chin and the easy droop of his wide shoulders. Here were two men who knew the hard realities of life, and were dismayed by nothing they knew.

Matonabbee turned and spoke quietly. The men dashed out their pipes and took up their muskets. One or two carried bows and arrows. The women picked up the thongs attached to the small sleds on which bundles of trade goods, food and extra clothing were securely lashed. Two small children ran ahead over the snow, while a tiny tot in a fur suit climbed on top of a load, calling to his mother, impatient to be off. On one sled reclined a silent woman, one of Matonabbee's wives too ill to walk. Two other women, also wives of Matonabbee, would pull the sled on which she lay.

With a last look at the stone walls of the fort above which

---

[1] Samuel Hearne, *A Journey* . . . , pp. 40, 41.

the flag waved gently in the light breeze, Hearne turned and walked away. Beside him strode Matonabbee, around them walked the other men. In single file behind came the sleds pulled by the women. Samuel Hearne was off on his epic walk in quest of a distant land where copper lay in sight on the ground, near the shore of a northern sea.

The plan which Hearne and Matonabbee had agreed upon was the very essence of simplicity. With an absolute minimum of personal gear, and only a few trade goods such as tobacco and ammunition, Hearne placed himself in the hands of Matonabbee saying, in effect, "Take me to the mouth of the Coppermine River." It is well to remember that only a certain kind of man could have taken such a step in the eighteenth century, a time when most Englishmen tended to be kings in the new lands they exploited. But Hearne had come up the hard way. He knew the realities of life and was sensible enough to realize that, away from the cosy world of the fort, an Indian such as Matonabbee would be the real leader of the expedition. Hearne's walk to the northwest would go down in history as his own. In fact, it was a venture in which Matonabbee was the leader, with Hearne as the follower and chronicler. In the days to come each man would play his part well.

Matonabbee's plan to take Hearne to the northern ocean was equally simple. They would walk northwest from Fort Prince of Wales, keeping just inside the northern edge of the bush where they could hunt deer for food and keep away from the vicious winter winds off the barren grounds to the north. Only when they were almost due south of the copper mines would they turn north and head for the sea. Matonabbee had set ideas on the composition of any party for such travel in the sub-Arctic lands of northern Canada. Central to his concepts was the use of women. That men should undertake long journeys without women was, to him, unthinkable, for:

... when all the men are heavy laden, they can neither hunt nor travel to any considerable distance; and in case they meet with success in hunting, who is to carry the produce of their labour? Women were made for labour; one of them can carry, or haul, as much as two men can do. They also pitch our tents, make and mend our clothing, keep us warm at night; and, in fact there is no such thing as travelling any distance, or for any length of time, in this country, without their assistance. Women, though they do every thing, are maintained at trifling expense; for as they always stand cook, the very licking of their fingers in scarce times, is sufficient for their sustenance.[2]

Matonabbee himself had five wives to look after his needs, and on the trip with Hearne he picked up three more en route.

All through the month of December Hearne walked steadily northwest at the side of Matonabbee. They travelled no set distance each day; everything depended on the condition of the snow, the state of the weather, the fullness or emptiness of their bellies. The group lived off the country, killing deer wherever they found them which meant "all feasting or all famine, sometimes too much, seldom just enough, frequently too little, and often none at all."[3] On good days they travelled as much as sixteen or eighteen miles; on bad days they made no progress at all, held in their tents by the bitter winds that swept whirling snow out of the north, cutting visibility to a few feet in every direction.

Day after day the small band plodded slowly northwest. They met few other Indians for the edge-of-tree country was thinly populated in midwinter. With those they did meet they shared food and talk, and then moved on. New Year's Eve, 1770, found Matonabbee very ill, the result of eating an enormous amount of deer meat following many days of short rations. But he soon recovered and the party pushed on. Early in January they arrived at the camp where the wives and children of those who

[2] *Ibid.,* p. 35.
[3] *Ibid.,* p. 21.

had not taken their families to the fort were living. The number in the expedition grew to nearly forty.

During February men and women suffered from frostbite, especially when crossing the open, wind-swept surfaces of the bigger lakes. Over the open ice the wind swept unhindered, sucking precious heat from their bodies, freezing exposed parts quickly. Several Indians were severely frostbitten on the face and hands. One woman froze her thighs and buttocks. Instead of sympathy she became the butt of much laughter from the other Indians because of her propensity to "shew a clean heel and good leg . . . which, though by no means considered here as bordering on indecency, is by far too airy to withstand the rigorous cold of a severe winter in a high Northern land."[4]

Early in March they reached Pike Lake, not far from the Dubawnt River. Here they found a camp of northern Indians living well from caribou they had caught and killed in a huge pound. As with everything he saw on his travels, Hearne described the pound:

> The pound is built by making a strong fence, with bushy trees. . . . not less than a mile around. . . . The entrance is not larger than a common gate, and the inside is so crowded with small counter-hedges as to very much resemble a maze; in every opening of which they set a snare, made with thongs of parchment deer-skins, well twisted together, which are amazingly strong. . . . a row of small brushwood is stuck up in the snow on each side of the entrance and continued along the open part of the lake, river or plain . . . in such a manner as to form two sides of a long, acute angle . . . growing gradually wider . . . from the entrance to the pound.

> When they see any deer going that way, men, women and children walk along the lake or riverside under the cover of the woods, till they get behind them, then step forthe into view, and proceed towards the pound in the form of a crescent. The poor timorous deer finding themselves pursued,

4 *Ibid.*, p. 48.

and at the same time taking the two rows of bushy poles to be two ranks of people . . . run straight forward until they get into the pound. The Indians then close in, and block up the entrance . . . the women and children walk around the pound to prevent them from breaking or jumping over the fence, while the men are employed spearing such as are entangled in the snares, or shooting with bows and arrows those which remain loose in the pound.[5]

In mid-April Matonabbee decided to camp for about two weeks in order to hunt deer, which were plentiful in the vicinity, and dry the meat to carry with them. The caribou would soon be moving out onto the barren grounds to the north on their annual spring migration and it would be harder to find deer in the northern fringe of the bush in the weeks ahead. Between hunts the Indians made small staves of birchwood, about one and one-quarter-inch square and seven to eight feet long, which would be used as tent poles for the summer camps on the treeless barrens, and as frame material for the snowshoes the following winter. They also collected birch bark and other wood, for the construction of the canoes which would be required for summer travel.

The meat and wood meant extra bundles to carry and haul. Fortunately by this time, because of the addition of Indian families en route, Hearne's expedition had grown to a total of about seventy people. Matonabbee solved some of his transportation problems by purchasing another wife from the northern Indians, bringing his total to eight, all of whom had ". . . in general, a very masculine appearance, yet he preferred them to those of a more delicate form and moderate stature."[6] Small wonder!

Late in April the group changed the general direction of march from northwest to almost due north. At the end of the first week in May, after much tedious foot-slogging through the

[5] *Ibid.*, pp. 49, 50.
[6] *Ibid.*, p. 56.

soft, melting snow of spring, they arrived at the small lake where they intended to build their canoes, and generally prepare themselves for summer travel on the barren grounds to the north. Here they were joined by more northern Indians until the party began to resemble a small army. There were over 200 people camped in the general area of the lake. Hearne was the only European and, as a stranger, was in some danger of his life, as the remote northern Indian groups thought little of robbing and turning out destitute anyone other than a member of their own group. But Matonabbee's presence, as Hearne's guide and protector, saved him from any such attack and Hearne took the precaution of distributing some of the tobacco and ammunition he had brought with him as presents for the Indians of the Coppermine River.

By mid-May the canoes had been made. Once again the expedition moved off. For the next two weeks Hearne and his group, augmented by about 100 northern Indians who had decided to go along, moved steadily northward, walking over the rotting ice of the lakes and rivers, continually wet to the skin in the hail, sleet and rain storms of spring. On the 28th of the month occurred a seemingly trivial event—one of Matonabbee's wives ran away, along with the wife of another hunter, presumably to return to husbands from whom they had been forcibly removed some time before. Matonabbee was greatly upset by this turn of events which was made even worse when, on the following day, a northern Indian by the name of Keelshies, who was one of the few people Hearne met who was bigger and stronger than Matonabbee, threatened to take another of Matonabbee's wives by force unless Matonabbee gave him ammunition and other articles he demanded. Matonabbee was forced to acquiesce to the demands.

These events almost spelled disaster for Hearne's expedition. Matonabbee was a very proud man. For him to have been humiliated in such a manner in front of his friend and companion was almost too much for him to bear; the blow to his pride and dignity was staggering. It was only after a great deal of persuasion and patient entreaty from Hearne that Matonabbee was dissuaded from giving up the plan to go north to the copper mines in favour of departing westward to a land where he knew the Indians better, and could count on being well-received by them. But he relented and agreed to continue on north.

When the northern Indians discovered that it was Hearne's intention to travel all the way to the sea, many hunters decided to go with him, hoping they would meet Eskimos on the coast whom they could kill and plunder for excitement and loot. As soon as Hearne became aware of their intentions he tried to discourage them from undertaking such a venture, but he was in no position to argue too strenuously. When he started north on the 1st of June his party consisted of about sixty people—his own group intact, plus a war party of northern Indians who left their women and children behind. Hearne was dismayed and horrified by this turn of events but he could do nothing to effect any change.

By the third week in June the ice had gone out of the lakes and rivers. Although they couldn't use the canoes for extended travel, as they were too small and too few in number, the party employed them to cross any open water they encountered. For the first time they met a band of Copper Indians and Hearne stopped to smoke a calumet of peace with the head man of the group. He found them to be friendly, and eager for the few trade goods that Hearne had brought from Fort Prince of Wales. They were intrigued by Hearne himself as he was the first European they had ever seen. They liked him as a person, they said, but did not think much of his white skin (". . . it resembled meat which had been sodden in water till all the blood was extracted.")[7] Whenever Hearne combed his blond hair one of the Indians was sure to gather up the loose hair and carefully wrap it for future closer inspection.

On the 1st of July Matonabbee and his Indians decided their

[7] *Ibid.*, p. 78.

wives and children should go no further. From now on they would travel as a war party of males. After they had killed enough deer to leave the women well-supplied with meat for two to three weeks the men started north. They had no problem finding the correct route, for many of the Copper Indians decided to tag along in the hope they would find a group of Eskimos to attack and plunder. The party crossed the Stoney Mountains with difficulty. Snow, sleet and rain kept them soaked to the skin most of the time, and on the warm, windless days they were tormented by thousands of mosquitoes that swarmed up from the damp ground.

On the 14th of July they reached the bank of the Coppermine River, some thirty miles from the sea. Hearne found the river to be quite different from the description usually given by Indians coming to Fort Prince of Wales, who reported it easily navigable by ships. Hearne found it to be narrow and turbulent, full of rapids and shoals, scarcely navigable for a large canoe. At the river the Indians killed several caribou and musk oxen, and then dried the meat to carry with them. As a war party they would do no more hunting in order not to alarm any Eskimos who might be camped ahead.

For two days they walked north while Hearne carefully surveyed the course of the river, still finding it full of rapids and falls. Early in the morning of July 16th scouts they had sent ahead returned with information of a camp of five Eskimo tents on the west bank of the river, about twelve miles ahead, at the foot of a great waterfall. Immediately the Indians crossed the river and began preparing their weapons for an attack.

The war party, with Hearne bringing up in the rear, moved carefully downstream, keeping under cover provided by deep ravines and valleys near the river edge. Close to the falls, they crept to the brink of a large hill and were able to look almost directly down on the Eskimo tents about 200 yards away, without being seen from below. They lay quietly, watching and waiting, painting their faces in hideous designs, plaiting their hair and fastening it high on their heads. In spite of the swarms of mosquitoes they removed most of their clothing until all were clad only in breech cloth and moccasins. Hearne watched, helpless to stop them, horrified at what he knew must soon take place.

By the time the Indians had made themselves thus completely frightful, it was near one o'clock in the morning of the seventeenth; when finding all the Eskimeaux quiet in their tents, they rushed forth from their ambuscade, and fell on the poor unsuspecting creatures, unperceived till close at the very eves of their tents, when they soon began the bloody massacre, while I stood neuter in the rear.

In a few seconds the horrible scene commenced; it was shocking beyond description; the poor unhappy victims were surprised in the midst of their sleep, and had neither time nor power to make any resistance; men, women and children, in all upward of twenty, ran out of their tents stark naked, and endeavoured to make their escape; but the Indians having possession of the landside, to no place could they fly for shelter. One alternative only remained, that of jumping into the river; but, as none of them attempted it, they all fell a sacrifice to Indian barbarity!

The shrieks and groans of the poor expiring wretches were truly dreadful; and my horror was much increased at seeing a young girl, seemingly about eighteen years of age, killed so near me, that when the first spear was stuck into her side she fell down at my feet. . . As two Indian men pursued this unfortunate victim, I solicited very hard for her life; but the murderers made no reply till they had stuck both their spears through her body, and transfixed her to the ground. Then they looked me sternly in the face, and began to ridicule me, by asking if I wanted an Esquimeaux wife; . . . . this butchery, cannot easily be conceived, much less described; though I summed up all the fortitude I was master of on the occasion, it was with difficulty that I could refrain from tears.

. . . we saw an old woman sitting by the side of the water, killing salmon, which lay at the foot of the fall as thick as a shoal of herrings. Whether from the noise of the fall, or a natural defect in the old woman's hearing, it is hard to determine, but certain it is, she had no knowledge of the tragical scene which had so lately been transacted at the tents, though she was not more than two hundred yards from the place. When we first perceived her, she seemed perfectly at ease, and was entirely surrounded with the produce of her labour. From her manner of behaviour and the appearance of her eyes, which were as red as blood, it is more than probable that her sight was not very good; for she scarcely discerned that the Indians were enemies, till they were within twice the length of their spears of her. It was in vain that she attempted to fly, for the wretches of my crew transfixed her to the ground in a few seconds, and butchered her in a most savage manner.

. . . the Northern Indians began to plunder the tents of the deceased of all the copper utensils they could find; such as hatchets, bayonets, knives, &c. after which they assembled on the top of an adjacent high hill, and standing all in a cluster, so as to form a solid circle, with spears erect in the air, gave many shouts of victory, constantly clashing their spears against each other.[8]

Almost 200 years after the massacre at Bloody Falls I stood, one bright July day, on the high rock bank of the Coppermine River where the rushing waters dash headlong through the narrow canyon carved in the solid rock of the low hills. Barely discernible at my feet was a circle of deeply imbedded stones, mute evidence of an Eskimo tent erected on this spot long ago. To my right, at the foot of the falls, was a wide gravel beach, at what must have been the exact spot on which the five Eskimo tents had been pitched. Immediately opposite where I stood was the hill behind which the Indians had painted their faces in readiness for the attack. Not fifty feet away was the little cove, with its small whirlpool, where the old woman had sat jigging for char in the moments before her horrible death.

[8] *Ibid.*, pp. 99-101.

Later in the day I stood on the hill behind the settlement of Coppermine. It was perhaps the same hill on which Samuel Hearne had stood in 1771 when he finally looked out over the frozen northern sea, the first European to reach this part of the north coast of America. Here, Hearne, ". . . after some consultation with the Indians, erected a mark, and took possession of the coast, on behalf of the Hudson's Bay Company."[9] As I looked out over the sandbars and open water of Coronation Gulf I wondered what Hearne must have felt on that day so long ago. He had reached his objective; he had proved there was no strait through central Canada. Because of this he must have felt a surge of pride and joy in his success. Yet only hours before he had witnessed the massacre of twenty helpless human beings, had left their mutilated bodies to lie on the banks of the river which had so recently given them life. Even Hearne, who had seen much of suffering and cruelty, must have been affected by this needless tragedy. Later in his life he would write: ". . . even at this hour I cannot reflect on the transactions of that horrid day without shedding copious tears."[10] In his moment of victory his heart must have been filled with sorrow at the price others had paid for his success.

Hearne walked back to Fort Prince of Wales to report the success of his mission. He went on to rise in the service of the Hudson's Bay Company, and eventually became Governor at Fort Prince of Wales. As Governor, in 1782, he had the unhappy experience of being forced to surrender the fort to La Pérouse, who carried Hearne captive to Europe. He was released along with his diaries, and in England he wrote his famous manuscript *A Journey from Prince of Wales's Fort, in Hudson's Bay, to the Northern Ocean*. On the 8th of October, 1792, he sold the manuscript for publication for the sum of £200. By that time Hearne was ill. Two weeks later he made his will and late

[9] *Ibid.*, p. 106.
[10] *Ibid.*, p. 100.

in November of the same year he died of dropsy at the age of forty-seven.

Hearne's friend, Matonabbee, returned with him to the fort and later became Chief of all the northern Indian groups. In the years following the expedition he continued to live as a hunter-trapper, each year bringing great quantities of fur to the fort, where he relished the chance to visit and talk with his friend. His last trip was in the spring of 1782, and he left intending to return in the winter. But that summer La Pérouse captured Fort Prince of Wales, and carried Hearne and the H.B.C. men off to Europe after blowing up sections of the fort's massive stone walls. When the news reached him at his hunting camp in the interior, Matonabbee hung his head in grief. He became a broken man. He could not bear to live after the calamity which had befallen his beloved Company and his equally beloved friend. In the winter of 1783 Matonabbee hanged himself in the bush. Six weeks later six of his wives and four of his children were dead of starvation in the northern bush.

Where Is the
Northwest Passage?

Thirty-six years after the death of Matonabbee, another great Indian Chief, Akaitcho, sat in a tent in the Canadian bush, north of Great Slave Lake. He was listening to Captain John Franklin attempt to explain why he wanted Akaitcho to guide him and his men to the mouth of the Coppermine River, from which point he wanted to explore and map the unknown coast eastward to Repulse Bay. After listening to Franklin's tale of the many men and ships sent out over 300 years in fruitless attempts to find the Northwest Passage, Akaitcho asked Franklin a simple question: "After all the searches, over all the years, if there is a Northwest Passage, why hasn't anyone been able to find it?"

Why indeed! Just where was this Northwest Passage which the early Arctic explorers could not find, but in the existence of which they so firmly believed?

Look at a full map of Canada with land reaching up to within 450 miles of the true North Pole. In the extreme north is the Arctic Ocean. As late as the nineteenth century many scholars believed that the centre of the Polar Sea was open water, free of ice the year round. This belief had its roots in the ancient myth of an aperture in the earth at the North Pole as described by Diaconus in the eighth century:

. . . and not far from where the shore which we before spoke of in the west, where the ocean extends without bounds, is that very deep abyss of the waters which we commonly call the Ocean's Navel. It is said twice a day to suck the waters into itself, and to spew them out again.[1]

In both the Arctic and Antarctic ships of the whalers and explorers frequently found areas of open water in very high latitude, fostering a belief in the minds of many that ice on the sea formed only in the vicinity of land. When I made my first trips to the Arctic, in the late 1940's, there was a good deal of argument among the people living along the west coast of Hudson Bay as to whether the centre of the bay froze over in the winter, an argument not finally settled until the overflights made by R.C.A.F. aircraft in the spring of 1950.[2]

The largest of the open water areas was thought to be in the region of the true North Pole. Today we know that the Arctic Ocean may well have been free of ice more than a million years ago, but within the time of written history it has been jammed with the massive floes of the main polar pack. We know also that heavy ice from this central mass, propelled by currents in the ocean, streams out through all the sea channels leading south to the north Atlantic Ocean. Polar ice clogs the north Greenland Sea. It jams the narrow opening of Kennedy Channel between Greenland and Ellesmere Island. It blocks the myriad channels between the northwestern Queen Elizabeth Islands. The main polar pack of the Arctic Ocean sends a continuous stream of massive ice east through the wide opening of M'Clure Strait into Melville Sound, and much of this ice flows southeast, down M'Clintock Channel, to smash against the northwest coast of King William Island deep in the central Arctic.

It is this flow of heavy ice through M'Clure Strait, Viscount Melville Sound and M'Clintock Channel that blocks the way

[1] From F. Nansen's, *In Northern Mists* . . . , p. 157.
[2] It does!

to swift summer sailing along the main sea channels to the north of the American continent. The new ice that forms each winter can stop ordinary ships for nine to ten months of the year. It can delay them during the two to three months of summer. It can even hold them prisoner for a year, sometimes two. But it cannot block the way indefinitely; sooner or later it must break up and move away, or it must melt away.

Not the massive, older ice from the polar sea. Not until it reaches the wide expanse of the north Atlantic Ocean, or the warmer waters of Queen Maud Gulf, does it begin to waste away and disappear. By its great mass it effectively blocks most of the main waterways over the roof of the world.

Look more closely at the map, at the maze of channels through the islands off the north Canadian coast. On the ordinary map it would appear that a number of sea routes exist by which ships could sail from the North Atlantic to the Beaufort Sea. In the east are the two main openings of Hudson Strait and Lancaster Sound. From Lancaster Sound it would seem that ships could sail west through the long channel of Lancaster Sound, Barrow Strait, Viscount Melville Sound and M'Clure Strait directly to the Beaufort Sea. Or they could turn south in Barrow Strait and sail through Peel Sound, Franklin Strait and Victoria Strait to Queen Maud Gulf, then west along the mainland coast to the Beaufort Sea. In the south it would appear that ships could sail from the North Atlantic through Hudson Strait to Foxe Channel and Foxe Basin, west through Fury and Hecla Strait to the Gulf of Boothia, then west again through narrow Bellot Strait, around the most northerly part of the North American continent, to Peel Sound.

But ordinary maps are deceiving; they do not show the ice cover on these northern sea channels. On all routes vessels can expect to meet, in summer, great masses of floating, one- and two-year-old ice. Both Bellot Strait and Fury and Hecla Strait are often plugged all summer long. Foxe Channel does not clear of ice until mid-August in most years. In 1958 I sailed on board

Of ice and sailing ships

Overleaf/Parry's ship, *Gripper,* sailing north off Greenland's coast through the sea ice and icebergs of Baffin Bay, July 1819.

a & b/ Parry's ship, *Hecla,* being towed from Hecla Cove, June 1827. Bay ice breaks up much later than ice in channels and early explorers often had to cut through the ice in the sheltered bays to get their ships to the open water offshore after wintering in the ice.

c/ Franklin's two canoes in the heavy seas of Coronation Gulf, off the north coast, August 1822.

d/ Parry's ships, *Hecla* and *Gripper,* frozen in at Winter Harbour, 1819-20, with their decks covered over for shelter.

e/ An artist's depiction of seamen attempting to free Franklin's ship, *Terror,* frozen immovably in the ice of Victoria Strait (prior to the abandonment of the ship and the subsequent loss of all men).

a

b

d

The explorer as artist

Many early Arctic explorers were artists or competent draughtsmen.

a/ Sometimes illustrations for the accounts of early explorers were done by artists in England. Note the Eskimo style dress but the man with the build of a European.

b/ Lake Athabaska, as Samuel Hearne saw it, 1771.

c & d/ Hood and Back recorded scenes from Franklin's trip to the north coast, such as dogs and sleds on Great Slave Lake, and boats of expedition on Hill River. In some cases, where latitude and longitude recorded by early explorers were inaccurate, sketches made by them have proved to be of great help in ascertaining the exact routes they followed.

a

b

c

d

a/ Fort Franklin on Great Bear
 Lake, Winter, 1826-7, prior to
 Franklin's second voyage along
 the coast.

b/ Fort Prince of Wales near
 present day Churchill on Hudson
 Bay, as it looked when Samuel
 Hearne was in residence as
 Chief Factor for the Hudson's
 Bay Company.

c/ Franklin's men portage a boat
 around rapids on his first
 journey from York Factory to the
 north coast, Summer, 1819.

d/ Franklin's men encounter hostile
 Eskimos at the mouth of the
 Mackenzie River during the
 second expedition along the
 north coast, Summer, 1827.

e/ Frobisher's battle with the
 Eskimos at Bloody Point in
 Frobisher Bay, second voyage,
 1877.

e

a/ The Franklin record, on standard Admiralty form, with the second message written in the margins. It was found by M'Clintock and is the only record known to exist from the last fatal expedition of Sir John Franklin.

b/ The signature of Samuel Hearne, carved into the rock of Sloop Cove near present day Churchill. It is one of the many still visible reminders of an era now past.

a

the Canadian Navy icebreaker, *H.M.C.S. Labrador*,[3] from Coral Harbour on Southampton Island north to Hall Lake on Melville Peninsula. Crisscrossing Foxe Channel and Foxe Basin the ship was in very heavy ice until a very few miles south of her destination. Sometimes the ice was so thick, and the press of wind and tide so heavy, that even the sturdy icebreaker was forced to heave to, to let the pressure subside before pushing north again.

The northern entrance through Lancaster Sound is navigable every summer, although drift ice can be met along its entire length. Sometimes this ice is heavy enough to stop ships in Barrow Strait. Other years they can sail right through to M'Clure Strait without seeing much ice. But in M'Clure Strait they come up against the main stream of heavy pack ice flowing southeast from the Arctic Ocean. Only rarely can ships expect to push their way through M'Clure Strait. Equally rarely can they expect to get through the Prince of Wales Strait to the southwest, although it was by this route that the experimental oil tanker, *Manhattan*, escorted by the Canadian icebreaker, *John A. Macdonald,* made her voyage through the Canadian sector of the Northwest Passage in the late summer of 1969.

Before the days of icebreakers, and cargo ships especially designed with double hulls of massive steel, there was only one practical waterway across the top of North America. This was the "mainland route": from the North Atlantic, up Davis Strait and Baffin Bay, then west through Lancaster Sound. From Barrow Strait the route was south into Peel Sound and Franklin Strait, then south*east* around behind King William Island, using its land mass as a shield against the heavy ice that streams down M'Clintock Channel to plug Victoria Strait, then west again through Simpson Strait and along the north coast of Canada to the Beaufort Sea, Bering Strait and the open water of the north Pacific Ocean. This was the waterway sought by the early

---

[3] This was before the *Labrador* was taken over by the Department of Transport, and later by the Canadian Coast Guard.

Arctic explorers, first as a possible route to the riches of Cathay, later as part of a great quest of geographic discovery in the northern lands of the world.

There were three main reasons why the early Arctic explorers were unable to find the passage: they were blinded by myth and misconception about the true diameter of the earth, about the nature of the polar waters, about the extent and position of the North American land mass; they came to the Arctic far too early in the season and left too soon, often just as the good sailing months of August and September were beginning; they had not developed a satisfactory wintering-over technique so as to be on the spot in the summer, ready to sail the moment the winter ice cleared. It wasn't until the early years of the nineteenth century that these errors and misconceptions began to be overcome and the second stage of exploration along the route of the Northwest Passage began.

Journey to the High Arctic

E dmonton Industrial Airport—one of the last mid-town airfields left in Canada—once *the* gateway to Canada's North. From this field, in the 1920's and 30's, flew the Fairchild and Fokker, Stinson and Junkers, Bellanca and Norseman, bush aircraft that opened up the vast northwestern Canadian hinterland and connected the remote settlements on the Peace, the Athabasca and the Mackenzie rivers with the south. Edmonton Industrial is the airport of Matt Berry, Wop May, Punch Dickins, Ernie Boffa, Stan McMillan, Doc Oaks; the bush pilots who helped write such a glorious chapter in the continuing history of aviation in Canada and establish themselves as legends in their own time.

From the apron in front of the small terminal building a Boeing 737 jet, Pacific Western Airlines Flight 773, eases out and begins to taxi for takeoff. The high-pitched whine of its engines drowns out the roar of traffic on the busy roads that now surround this mid-town airport. Slowly the big jet lumbers past the Turbo-Beavers and Twin Otters, aging DC 3's and DC 6's, fat Hercules transports and sleek business jets, all modern successors to the famous bush planes of an age now past. At 8:00 p.m. on a warm August evening, PWA Flight 773 is ready to take off on its twice weekly run north to Resolute, on Cornwallis Island in Canada's High Arctic, farthest north post of call for any regularly scheduled airline in the world.[1]

The takeoff is smooth. Quickly the rows of houses and apartments slide beneath the wing and the plane climbs steeply above range land and scattered bush. In a few minutes almost all sign of civilization has been left behind. The 737 is flying high over the sub-Arctic bush of northern Alberta, once Mecca of the fur trade, now an Eldorado of natural gas and oil. High over Wood Buffalo Park it flies, over scattered herds of buffalo that inhabit this northern sanctuary, some of the last remnants of the millions of animals that once roamed free over the immense inland plains of North America.

At 33,000 feet the plane crosses the sixtieth parallel, border between Alberta and the Northwest Territories, and flies on over the huge open pit of the zinc-lead mine at Pine Point. Ahead, the wide expanse of Great Slave Lake shimmers in the dull light of late evening in a far north land. Just visible off the port wing is the wide channel of the Mackenzie, longest river in Canada, called by Alexander Mackenzie in 1789 "River of Disappointment" because it failed to lead him to the western sea. Slowly the plane lets down over the lake. Beneath, a small tug pushing a single barge leaves a long white wake on the blue water. The plane banks right. Bare rock and bush slide by, and suddenly, out of nowhere, there appears the rectangular outlines of a small city—streets, homes, stores, offices, apartment buildings—nestled among the rocks on the north shore of the lake. The plane drops swiftly to a smooth landing at Yellowknife, capital of the Northwest Territories, gold centre of the Canadian North.

The stopover is brief. An hour after landing the plane is off again, climbing north over the scrub bush and rock of the Canadian Shield. High above the lakes and rivers traversed with so

[1] Nordair, flying out of Montreal, also has a scheduled flight to Resolute, via Frobisher Bay and Hall Beach on Melville Peninsula.

much labour by Matonabbee and Samuel Hearne, the jet wings steadily northward, gradually leaving behind the patchy tree growth to fly over the great inland prairie, called by some the Barren Ground, that sweeps in unbroken splendour to the northern coast of Canada and the islands beyond. Over the caribou herds of Contwoyto Lake, over the musk oxen of Bathurst Inlet, across the Arctic Circle and out over the north coast of continental America the plane wings its way. The direction of flight is north by northeast and the time is near midnight, yet the sun shines directly into the cockpit in this land of the midnight sun. Flight 773 takes almost twenty-four hours to fly the 3,100 miles from Edmonton to Resolute Bay and return. During all that time the sun circles endlessly around the sky, while in midwinter the plane flies the same path without seeing the sun at all.

Far beneath, the massive white ice floes of M'Clintock Channel reflect the red rays of the low lying sun. Prince of Wales Island drifts by, the largest completely uninhabited island in the world. Over the ice-dotted waters of Barrow Strait the plane lets down again. In a few minutes it bounces slightly and the airframe vibrates from the gravel under the dual wheels. Flight 773 taxies to a stop at the refueling pumps of the northern air base of Resolute Bay.

Resolute Bay isn't like Frobisher Bay on Baffin Island, or Churchill on Hudson Bay. It isn't a settlement or a small town, although there is an Eskimo village on the seashore nearby. Resolute is a gas station for aircraft, a supply base supporting the far-flung weather stations and research bases scattered throughout the islands to the west and north, and the exploration crews drilling for oil in the High Arctic islands. First established as a small, joint Canadian-American weather station in 1947, it was later enlarged by the Royal Canadian Air Force and operated as a services air base. On April 1, 1964, the Department of Transport[2] took over the operation as a civilian

[2] Now known as the Ministry of Transport

airfield. Although remote from the centres of civilization in the south, Resolute is as busy as any international airport in Canada. Although its traffic does not include sleek DC 8's or DC 9's, it bustles with stubby Hercules freighters, cargo-crammed DC 3's and DC 6's, STOL Twin Otters and Helio Couriers, helicopters of all sizes that come and go at any time of the day or night.

Resolute is unlike Churchill or Frobisher Bay in another way. Except for the ruins of a few old Thule Eskimo houses on a nearby shore, it has no relics of past history, no forts, no explorers' caches, no old cairns, no wrecks of ships, not even an old grave with a bleached wooden headboard to mark the passing of a sailor of long ago. History has left marks all through the Arctic Island but none at Resolute. When the ships sailed into Lancaster Sound in 1947 with the men and material for the base, their destination was Winter Harbour on Melville Island, far to the west of Cornwallis Island, and an historic location in the Arctic Islands. But, like Martin Frobisher's fleet almost 400 years before, the ships ran into bad ice conditions. They were unable to reach Winter Harbour and the materials for the weather station were put ashore at Resolute. This was the first time that anyone other than Eskimos had ever settled on this lonely shore.

But history in Arctic Canada is never far away. Walk southeast along the coast of Cornwallis Island for a few miles, climb the scree slopes of the first high hill you come to and stand on the rounded top of broken shale, turn your back to the midnight sun shining low on the northern horizon, and look south over the ice-dotted waters of Barrow Strait. To your left the strait flows east to become Lancaster Sound, eastern gateway to Baffin Bay, Davis Strait and the north Atlantic. On your right it runs west, widening out to become Viscount Melville Sound, then on to M'Clure Strait. Beyond this lies the ice-clogged waters of the Arctic Ocean. Across Barrow Strait to the southwest is the wide opening of Peel Sound leading south, through Franklin and James Ross straits, to the open water of Rae Strait. From this hilltop at Resolute you look out over the major water channels of the Northwest Passage waterway across the top of America, channels that took the early Arctic explorers nearly 200 years to find.

The ships of almost every major expedition to northern Canada sailed through the waterway before you, including, in 1969, the huge *Manhattan* and her escort the *John A. Macdonald*.

Past here in 1819 sailed the *Hecla* and *Gripper* of Edward Parry. He was the first explorer to navigate west from Baffin Bay, first to site the island on which you stand, and first to reach western Melville Island and win a British Admiralty award of £5,000 for himself and his crew. But he was then defeated in his attempts to sail to the Beaufort Sea.

In 1829 the *Victory* of John Ross came to Lancaster Sound, first and last paddle-steamer ever to voyage to the Canadian Arctic. Her hull was left to bleach on the lonely east coast of Boothia Peninsula, while Ross and his crew escaped in the ship's boats to Lancaster Sound, and then in a whaling ship back across the Atlantic.

In 1845 the *Erebus* and the *Terror* of John Franklin sailed by here, to circumnavigate Cornwallis and prove that it was an island. They spent the winter frozen in at Beechey Island, about fifty miles east of where you stand, before sailing south through Peel Sound to vanish forever from the sight of man. The loss of their crews added 129 more names to the roll of men lost in the white wilderness of Arctic Canada.

Past this point sailed many ships on Franklin search expeditions. In 1849 the *Enterprise* and *Investigator* of James Clark Ross worked their way through heavy ice in Barrow Strait only to drift back again, helplessly trapped in massive ice floes, not to be released until well out in Baffin Bay. In 1850 the four ships of Horatio T. Austin were forced to winter in the ice of Barrow

Strait off Griffith Island, about five miles offshore from the present airfield at Resolute. In 1852, five ships—the *Assistance, Pioneer* and *North Star* under Edward Belcher; the *Intrepid* and *Resolute* under Henry Kellett—sailed through Barrow Strait. They failed to find Franklin and, two years later, four of the ships were abandoned on order of Belcher who considered them helplessly beset in polar ice. Three of them were never seen again but the massive hull of the especially-built *Resolute* refused to die. Trapped in heavy ice the empty ship drifted west through Lancaster Sound and south across Baffin Bay into Davis Strait, where she was found by Captain Buddington of the whaler *George Henry*. Captain Buddington put a crew on board his prize and sailed the sturdy *Resolute* to New London in Connecticut. The American government bought the ship, refitted it completely, then returned it to England as a gift. When the *Resolute* was finally broken up in 1878 Queen Victoria ordered a desk to be made from stout oak timbers of the hull and the desk was sent across the Atlantic to President Rutherford Hayes of the U.S.A. This was the desk used by the late President John F. Kennedy until his tragic death by assassination in the autumn of 1963.

The air base at Resolute is named after this stout vessel. Many geographic features in the Canadian Arctic honour ships that have sailed to this far north land: Fury and Hecla Strait, Investigator Point, Discovery Bay, Resolution Island, Prince Albert Sound. Some honour the explorers themselves: M'Clintock Channel, Parry Islands, Back River, M'Clure Strait, District of Franklin. Still other names pay tribute to men and women who gave moral and financial support: Victoria Island, Lancaster Sound, Prince Regent Inlet, Lady Ann Strait, Cornwallis Island, Boothia Peninsula, Lady Franklin Islands. There are even some to remind us of the government agency responsible for most of the sailing expeditions: Navy Board Inlet, Admiralty Inlet, Committee Bay. Although merchants and princes made possible most discoveries in the Canadian Arctic during the seventeenth and eighteenth centuries, by the nineteenth, leadership in Arctic exploration had passed to the British Navy.

In the early years of the nineteenth century there were sound business, political and scientific reasons for resuming the search for a Northwest Passage. Many in England felt it necessary to counteract the growing Russian expansion across the Pacific and into Alaska (then an extension of Russia onto the American continent). But the real impetus came from the initiative of three men, each of whom had good reason for pushing continued Arctic exploration. In 1817 William Scoresby Jr., son of the founder of the famous Whitby whaling firm and himself a whaling captain, reported to the British Admiralty that for two years past his ships had sailed through ice-free waters as far north as eighty degrees latitude in seas that were usually covered with thick ice. He suggested the time might be right for the discovery of a Northwest Passage and for a voyage across the supposedly "open" polar sea to Asia. Sir Joseph Banks, President of the Royal Society, was delighted to push for a resumption of such voyages, as this would open up new areas of the world's surface to scientific investigation. Sir John Barrow, Secretary of the Admiralty, who had a personal interest in the Arctic as a result of a voyage with the whaling fleet to Spitsbergen waters, had on his hands dozens of ships, plus hundreds of sailors and officers with little to do (following the banishment of Napoleon to the island of St. Helena).

Thus it was that the British Navy began its series of Arctic voyages into the Canadian North. Manned by young navy veterans, captained by vigorous young officers eager for fame and glory, presided over by men of vision who looked out across the seas that surrounded their tiny island kingdom, the ships of the British Navy sailed west and north to lay the ghost of the open polar sea, and to finally solve the riddle of the Northwest Passage.

Who Was Edward Parry?

John Davis was the first English sailor to probe the corridor between Greenland and the Canadian Arctic Islands. During three voyages (1585, 1586, 1587) he discovered his strait and charted sectors of the west coast of Greenland and the east coast of Baffin Island as far north as Cape Dyer. He sailed into Cumberland Sound for a short distance and thought it might be a strait.

In 1616, William Baffin, with Robert Bylot as ship's master, the same Bylot of Henry Hudson fame, made one of the great Arctic voyages in that early age of sail. In the *Discovery*, Hudson's old vessel, Baffin navigated north to latitude seventy-seven degrees twenty-two minutes in the upper end of Baffin Bay, charting major portions of the east coasts of Ellesmere, Devon and Baffin islands. He noted the entrances to the three major waterways that penetrate the High Arctic islands (Smith Sound, Jones Sound and Lancaster Sound), although he thought all three were enclosed bays. Baffin landed on the east coast of Devon Island to become the first European to set foot in the High Arctic islands of Canada.[1] Unfortunately his carefully drawn maps were discredited in England. Few believed that he had been in the regions he claimed to have discovered. Two hundred years later maps of the

---

[1] Only Eskimos and Norse from Greenland had been there before him.

Arctic coast of America were still being produced showing a great bay between Greenland and Baffin Island, with a huge extension on its northern side on which was written: "Baffin's Bay, according to the relation of W. Baffin, 1616, but not now believed." It wasn't until the voyage of John Ross in 1818 that Baffin's charts were found to have been correct, and the true outlines of these Arctic coasts were restored to the maps of the day.

John Ross' voyage of 1818 marked the beginning of the new British thrust into the north. In that year a two-pronged expedition was despatched by the Navy; the *Dorothea* and *Trent*, under David Buchan, were sent to search for a route northward across the "open" polar sea; the *Isabella* and *Alexander*, under Ross, followed Baffin's trail into Davis Strait and Baffin Bay. Among the officers of the four vessels were names destined to become famous over the next twenty-five years: James Clark Ross, Frederick Beechey, George Back, Edward Parry and John Franklin. Franklin was second in command to David Buchan; Parry, second in command to John Ross.

John Ross must go down in history as one of the most unfortunate explorers ever to have sailed to Arctic Canada. The first of the British captains to head an expedition to the Arctic following the defeat of Napoleon at Waterloo, he should have covered himself with glory. Instead he earned only the hostility of his fellow officers, and the contempt of his superiors in England. For Ross made the same mistake Baffin had made 200 years before: he saw Smith Sound, Jones Sound and Lancaster Sound as enclosed bays.[2] In Lancaster Sound he sailed the *Isabella* west for about forty miles before he thought he saw a row of mountains blocking its western end. His report to the Admiralty was at variance with statements made by his junior

[2] This was not the last time Ross made a similar mistake. In 1829, he sailed south into Prince Regent Inlet and passed across the mouth of Brentford Bay without seeing the opening of Bellot Strait. He returned to England after accomplishing much in the way of scientific investigation, but without realizing he had sailed right past the opening he sought.

officers who stated publicly that they had seen no sign of land blocking Lancaster Sound:

> . . . we could not see anything like land at the bottom of the inlet, nor was the weather well calculated at the time for seeing any object at a great distance it being somewhat hazy.[3]

The glory that could have been Ross' went instead to his second in command, Edward Parry. While careful not to criticize his superior directly in public, Parry convinced the Admiralty that he had seen no land blocking Lancaster Sound, and that he firmly believed this to be the route of the Northwest Passage waterway. Parry was strongly supported by Sir John Barrow who treated Ross with disdain. A new expedition was planned to depart in the summer of 1819, provisioned for a two-year stay in the Arctic, and Parry was given the command.

William Edward Parry was one of the great Arctic explorers of his age and it is not hard to understand why he was to succeed where John Ross had failed. Contrast the philosophy of the cautious Ross:

> . . . it is imprudent, as well as idle, to be perpetually pushing on to reach every track of open water, unless it can be done without risk, and unless also there be a prospect of retaining the ground that has been gained.[4]

with that of the resourceful Parry:

> To push forward while there is any open water to enable us to do so, had uniformly been our first endeavour; it has not been until the channel has actually terminated, that we have been accustomed to look for a place of shelter, to which

[3] Edward Parry, *Memoirs of Rear-Admiral Sir Edward Parry* (London: Longmans, 1857), p. 93.
[4] Sir John Ross, *Narrative of a Second Voyage in Search of a Northwest Passage* (London: Webster, 1835), 2 vols., p. 179.

the ships were then conducted with all possible despatch; and I may safely venture to predict that no ship acting otherwise will ever accomplish the Northwest Passage.[5]

Parry was born in the city of Bath on December 19, 1790, a time of great change in England and the rest of the western world. The Industrial Revolution was reshaping the face of Britain, changing what had been a pastoral and agricultural society into a complex of industrial cities. King George III was slowly going mad and the power of government was falling more and more onto the shoulders of the Prime Minister, William Pitt, and Parliament. Only one year before, the French people had risen up in arms against their King, had stormed the Bastille in Paris and set in motion all the wild excesses of the French Revolution. Seven years before, Britain had recognized the independence of the United States of America.

Parry was the youngest of nine children, son of a doctor who had done well enough to purchase an estate called "Summer Hill," where he became a country gentleman in the fashion of the times. Brought up in a relaxed household, attended by servants, surrounded by the small luxuries of a nineteenth-century, upper-middle-class home, young Parry evolved into an affable, outgoing boy, good at athletics, and a promising scholar. His parents planned that he should follow in the footsteps of his father but, in 1803, a patient of Parry's father, the niece of Admiral William Cornwallis, Commander-in-Chief of the Channel Fleet, recommended Parry to her uncle. On June 30, 1803, Edward Parry joined the navy ship, *Ville de Paris* as a Volunteer of the First Class. He was only twelve years old.

These were difficult times for the British Navy. France controlled most of Europe. The British held command of the sea from Scotland south to the tip of Africa 6,000 miles away, blockading French ports, ready to defend against threatened invasion

[5] Sir William Edward Parry, *Journal of a Third Voyage for the Discovery of a Northwest Passage* (London: Murray, 1826), p. 148.

across the Channel. On board the ships English sailors lived like animals. Recruited by the infamous press gangs which roamed the country seizing any able-bodied man they could find, seamen spent months cooped up on ships that rarely fought anyone, didn't go anywhere, that were constantly battered by wind and storm at their lonely stations off the blockaded ports. They lived in cramped quarters where it was impossible to stand upright. They ate the monotonous diet of salt pork, bad cheese and hard biscuits, washed down with foul water. They were punished for the slightest infraction of rules, strung up on the yardarm, or flogged at the masthead. One thousand lashes was not unusual, and was followed by salt rubbed into the open wounds—if the man were still alive.

Six years before Parry joined the Navy the sailors had staged the biggest mutiny ever to take place on the sea. Angered by the conditions under which they were forced to serve, driven to despair by the fact that they had not been paid for months (in 1797 the Navy owed ships' crews some fourteen million dollars in back pay), they struck. The mutiny lasted for months and before it was over 50,000 mutineers controlled more than 100 fighting ships, right in the middle of the war with France. The mutineers lost, and thirty-five of their leaders were hanged. But in the end they won, for Britain slowly began to improve the lot of her tars. When Parry joined the Navy in 1803 conditions on the ships had begun to improve, but service on a British naval vessel still meant a long, lonely vigil on blockade stations in stormy seas, relieved only by the occasional skirmish with the enemy. Parry never forgot the miserable lot of the British seaman. When he achieved command of his own vessel he wrote home to his family:

> You will be glad to hear that both our ships are completely manned, and as well manned as any ships that ever went to sea. Besides our own men, we have had the choice of a great many of Captn. Buchan's and Franklin's, so that we have had every possible advantage of selection. Good wages, good feed-

ing, and good treatment are not always to be had, poor fellows! and as we bear a tolerably good character in these respects, we have been quite overwhelmed with volunteers.[6]

Parry did well on the *Ville de Paris* and was promoted to midshipman. After the great victory at Trafalgar he spent another two years with the Channel Fleet, and was then transferred to the command of a small gunboat which fought Danish gunboats that harried the English convoys in the Baltic Sea. In 1810 he was commissioned as a lieutenant on the frigate *Alexandria* and had his first experience in Arctic waters as part of the squadron protecting the Greenland and Spitsbergen whaling fleets. While there he became interested in the study of the stars and in naval surveying, and did well enough in both fields to publish pamphlets and charts. In 1813 he was transferred to the North American Station where he took part in the blockade of the American coast, and went on a successful raid up the Connecticut River which earned him a bar to his general service medal.

In 1813 the war in Europe and America came to an end and Lieutenant Edward Parry was faced with the unpleasant prospect of languishing as a half-pay naval officer. For a while he remained on active duty with the North American Fleet. In 1816 he was First-Lieutenant on the *Niger* when that ship sailed to Quebec as escort for the new Governor-General of Canada, Sir John Sherbrooke. Then, in 1817, his father died, and Parry returned to England to be with his family.

While still on station in North America he had applied for a position on an expedition to the Congo but had reached England too late to go. Not long after his return he noticed an item in a newspaper announcing the northern naval expedition that John Ross would command. Parry wrote to a friend of his father's stating that, in exploring, "he was ready for hot or cold."[7] His letter came to the attention of Sir John Barrow who

[6] Ann Parry, *Parry of the Arctic* (London: Chatto & Windus, 1963), p. 46.
[7] *Ibid.*, p. 28.

"was so pleased with the letter, and the little treatise that accompanied it [Parry's published treatise on nautical astronomy], that he at once submitted to Lord Melville his opinion that he was just the man for such an appointment."[8] In this way did Edward Parry begin his career as an explorer. He sailed as second in command to John Ross in 1818, and then went on to command his own vessel and become the foremost ice navigator of his time.

[8] *Ibid.*

Farthest West

Darkness came early on the late winter day. One by one the great flambeaux flared up to cast yellow, flickering light over the massive hull standing naked in the stocks of the great naval yard at Deptford on the Thames. All day shipwrights and joiners had scrambled over the ship, as they had done for weeks past, and as they would do for two months into spring, filling the air with clatter of mallet and adze, and with raucous voices that cursed a stubborn plank or dowel, or sang a lusty song of the sea. Far into the night they toiled, reshaping the ship from a vessel of war into a craft of discovery. They doubled the planking on the hull and inserted a layer of felt for insulation; they reinforced the keel to withstand the forward drive through scattered ice; they sharpened the set of the bow for probing between massive floes; they changed the rigging to that of a barque, like the whaling ships, for easier handling among the shifting ice.

> The *Hecla* will be a charming ship. I really believe she will combine everything we want—great strength, capacity of hold, good sailing, and fine accommodation for Officers and Men. The Arrangement of Cabins, Masts, Rigging, and indeed everything that can contribute to my own and other's comfort, and to the good of the Service, is left entirely to myself.[1]

[1] *Ibid.*, p. 44.

So wrote Lieutenant William Edward Parry on the evening of January 21, 1819, as he sat in his lodgings at Number 3 Downing Street in London, writing to his family in Bath. That day Parry had commissioned the *Hecla*, a former bomb ship, and the smaller gun-brig, *Gripper*, in preparation for the voyage of discovery into the Arctic seas that he was to command.

> Promotion must not be expected; as it seems Lord M.[2] has set his face against it. But, when I look at the *Hecla*, and the chart of Lancaster's Sound, oh! what is promotion to these.[3]

The British Naval officers who were to sail north across unknown Arctic seas over the next quarter of a century were very different men from the flamboyant Martin Frobisher and the reticent Samuel Hearne. Reared as English, Irish and Scottish gentlemen, aloof from the bitter class struggles that were shaking Britain to its core, moulded and stereotyped in the traditions of England's senior fighting service in which every man was expected to do his duty for King and country, they took on the challenge of the Northwest Passage as a supreme test of individual luck, courage, knowledge and skill, and produced what has been called the "golden age of Arctic exploration." Every age must have its popular heroes; in the nineteenth century the Arctic explorers of the British Navy filled this role.

> *But fairer England greets the wanderer now,*
> *Unfaded laurels shade her Parry's brow:*
> *And on the proud memorials of her fame*
> *Lives, linked with deathless glory, Franklin's name.*[4]

These men sought no riches of Cathay. They sought glory for England and knighthood for themselves. Most achieved their

---

[2] Lord Melville, First Lord of the Admiralty
[3] Ann Parry, *Parry of the Arctic*, pp. 44, 45.
[4] Capt. A. H. Markham, *Life of Sir John Franklin* (London, 1891), p. 172.

goal to become elder statesmen in the Arctic Council of England: Sir Edward Parry, Sir George Back, Sir James Clark Ross, Sir Edward Sabine, Sir John Richardson, Sir John Franklin are names of men who knew the Arctic well. Long before Canada came into being as a nation these men sailed from England to set down on the maps, for the first time, the outlines of the Arctic islands and the northwest coast of North America.

We had a charming party to dine with us yesterday; Mrs, Browne and her family, with Sabine[5] himself. The day was delightful. I took them on board the *Gripper*, and then down to Greenwich Hospital and the Park. We sang the Canadian Boat-Song, as we rowed down the Thames, and after walking to the top of the Hill in the Park on which the Observatory stands, and admired the lovely view from there for a while, returned on board at half past five.[6]

On April 13th Parry reported the ships ready to sail. But for almost a month he waited for the fair wind that would carry the *Hecla* and *Gripper* down the Thames. The delay proved to be not unpleasant; the weather was fine and the officers visited in town or dined on board with invited guests.

These visits are peculiarly interesting to those who have relations going out, and I feel a great pleasure in promoting them. Lady Beechey and her family, making a party of eleven, (Sir William[7] included) did the same the day before, and were very much gratified. . . . I amused my party yesterday very much by putting my life preserver on Miss Browne, and making her blow it up, or inflate it, herself![8]

A few years later Parry would not be so amused by Miss Browne. Before he left England he came to some sort of an

---

[5] Capt. Edward Sabine, R.A., astronomer on the *Hecla*, later Sir Edward Sabine, President of the Royal Society

[6] Ann Parry, *Parry of the Arctic*, p. 48.

[7] The famous artist who painted Parry's portrait

[8] Ann Parry, *Parry of the Arctic*, p. 48.

"understanding" with the young lady, but continued absence in the polar region cooled the affair. Miss Browne's mother considered that Parry had dishonourably broken off an engagement, and her innuendo caused Parry much pain, particularly after the circulation of a humorous jingle, after the fashion of the times.

Parry, why this dejected air?
Why are your looks so much cast down?
None but the Brave deserve the Fair,
Anyone may have the Browne!

But his discomfort soon passed. Parry discovered that Miss Browne had not been as true as he had supposed, and that she was engaged to someone else during his absence. It wasn't long before another charming young lady began to eradicate the memory of the flighty Miss Browne.

A fair wind never did arrive; both the *Hecla* and *Gripper* had to be towed by paddle-steamer down river. It was May 11th before the two ships stood out to sea and turned their bows towards the north. By mid-June they had rounded Cape Farewell, the southern tip of Greenland, and were sailing north through Davis Strait. To port, Parry could see the long line of towering icebergs that marked the eastern edge of the pack ice covering the central waters of Davis Strait and Baffin Bay. It stretched all the way north to seventy-five degrees of latitude, and was the main ice barrier that had to be crossed or bypassed in order to reach Lancaster Sound. Parry planned to force his ships through the 100-mile-wide mass of ice in Davis Strait in a bold attempt to cross directly to the Baffin Island shore. Turning west he took the *Hecla* and *Gripper* directly into the floes.

He didn't get far. For a week the ships were helplessly beset, drifting south for fifteen miles before Parry was able to extricate both vessels. As a result of this experience he decided to sail north, through the more or less open water along the west coast of Greenland, and cross Baffin Bay at a higher latitude.

For three weeks Parry headed the *Hecla* and *Gripper* north, with the pack ice a familiar sight off the port rail, and Greenland's ice cap on the horizon to starboard. Weather alternated between storms that set the sea ice and huge icebergs in violent motion, and dead calms with sky clouded by thick mists that froze into hoarfrost on the masts and rigging so thick it had to be shaken and scraped off each morning before the ships could raise sail. They met only one other vessel on this coast, the whaler *Brunswick*, from Hull, whose master signalled, by striking a broom handle smartly on the deck nineteen times, that her hold contained a full cargo of whales. Not until the ships reached latitude seventy-three degrees north, almost opposite the entrance to Lancaster Sound, did Parry again take them into the ice. This time he was determined to force a way through. Only later did whalers discover the famous "North Water" in northern Baffin Bay, an ice-free area in the early summer, through which ships can sail with relative ease.

The heavier *Hecla* went first, opening a channel for the slower and clumsier *Gripper*. Once well into the ice Parry found there was little wind and little open water, although the pack ice was laced with narrow openings. Anchors were put out on the ice and the vessels pulled forward by the ships' capstans. Often they had to be tracked along with hawsers pulled by the crew on the ice. This work exhausted the sailors and Parry saw to it that "a dram be given to each man as soon as he came back on board and put on dry clothes, taking care that none were allowed to have it, till they had done so."[9] In this way they worked the two ships through eighty miles of pack ice until, at the end of July, they found themselves in open water on the west side of Baffin Bay. On August 2nd the *Hecla* and *Gripper* stood in the entrance of Lancaster Sound, with a strong east wind heeling them down as they moved steadily through the ice-free waters.

This was the moment of truth for Parry. What lay ahead?

[9] *Ibid.*, p. 51.

Was Lancaster Sound a landlocked bay, as both Baffin and Ross had claimed? Or was this the channel through to Bering Strait?

> We were now about to enter and explore that great sound or inlet which has obtained a degree of celebrity beyond which it might otherwise have been considered to possess, from the very opposite opinions which have been held with regard to it. . . . It is more easy to imagine than describe the oppressive anxiety which was visible on every countenance, while, as the breeze increased to a fresh gale, we ran quickly to the Westward. The Mastheads were crowded by the Officers the whole afternoon and evening, and an observer who could quietly have looked, would have been amused to see the eagerness with which the report of everyone just come down from the crow's nest was received.[10]

Parry pressed all sail on the *Hecla*, leaving the slower *Gripper* with instructions to rendezvous on the eighty-fifth meridian, if the way ahead should prove to be clear. Westward the ship flew over the water, with no sign of land ahead. On through the "mountains" of John Ross, on past the two southern openings of Navy Board and Admiralty Inlet (which they discovered and named), on to the place of rendezvous with the *Gripper* where they waited for that ship to come up, then on still farther went the *Hecla* and *Gripper* together, sailing through a wide channel, completely free of ice. With every passing mile their hopes for a passage through to the western sea grew stronger. Anxiety and tension gave way to gaiety and laughter. Parry noted that as the water was

> . . . the usual oceanic colour, and a long swell was rolling in from the south and east, some of the most sanguine among us had calculated the bearing and distance of Ice Cape, Alaska, as a matter of no very difficult or improbable accomplishment.[11]

[10] *Ibid.*, pp. 29, 31.
[11] *Ibid.*, p. 34.

Parry himself carefully marked the discoveries on his charts and reserved judgement as to what the future might bring.

He was wise. On the evening of August 4th a thin white line appeared ahead. As the ships drew closer Parry could see nothing but solid ice fields stretching north and south across the water. Off Maxwell Bay, on the coast of Devon Island, the two ships were forced to turn south and run along the edge of the ice. They saw schools of white whales, and narwhal, the latter called sea-unicorns by the sailors because of their long, spirally-grooved tusks. But no way through could be found. From Maxwell Bay to Cape Clarence the strait was blocked with solid ice.

Although disappointed, Parry was not dismayed by this turn of events. The Arctic sailing season was just beginning and he was doubly sure now that Lancaster Sound would lead him to the western sea. While waiting for the ice to clear he took the *Hecla* and *Gripper* south into another wide, open-water channel between Baffin Island and a land he later named North Somerset (Somerset Island), after his native county. At latitude seventy-one degrees, fifty-three minutes in the waterway which he later named Prince Regent Inlet, the ships were stopped by solid ice. Parry named the promontory to his left Cape Kater, and turned back to Lancaster Sound. He didn't know that he was almost directly opposite the opening of Bellot Strait, the narrow waterway around the most northerly part of the continent of North America.

It was late in August before the ice in Lancaster Sound began to move. It vanished overnight. The way west was open. Past Devon Island they sailed, noting tiny Beechey Island in passing, and across the wide opening of an ice-free strait that led off to the north, which Parry named Wellington Channel. The land on the west side of this waterway he called Cornwallis after "my first naval friend and patron."[12] New discoveries were coming

[12] Sir William Edward Parry, *Journal of a Voyage for the Discovery* . . . (London: Murray, 1821), p. 52.

so thick and fast that Parry began to run out of names. After honouring many of the great he named minor features after friends and relatives: Cape Herschel, Benjamin Hobhouse Inlet, Cape Eardley Wilmot.

For some time Parry had found his compasses so sluggish as to be useless for navigation. The ships were sailing in close proximity to the North Magnetic Pole, then situated on Boothia Peninsula.[13] Without the compasses he had to navigate by steering the ships on each other when out of sight of land. In thick fogs he moved ahead by the feel of the wind, plus constant use of the sounding chains. In Barrow Strait, scattered bands of pack ice slowed progress somewhat, but Parry had no difficulty working the ship through. On September 4th the ships passed the meridian of 110 degrees west longitude and earned for their crews the £5,000 reward offered by the Admiralty to those British subjects who first crossed this line, north of the Arctic Circle. Parry's share of the prize would be £1,000. In honour of the event he called a nearby headland, Cape Bounty.

The *Hecla* and *Gripper* continued to beat their way west along the south shore of Melville Island. A headland, which Parry thought to be on the same meridian at which Samuel Hearne had reached the mouth of the Coppermine River, was named Cape Hearne in honour of the first man to walk overland to the northern sea.[14] On September 6th the ships rounded Cape Providence. Temperatures now fell at night to near zero and new ice was forming on the sea. With the season far advanced in this high north latitude, Parry still had hopes of sailing through to open water in the west, but the ships were running into fields of heavy ice which pressed them close in on the steeply shelving shore. The mountainous floes of this main ice

---

[13] The Magnetic Poles shift constantly, and even disappear at times. The present position of the North Magnetic Pole is on Bathurst Island.

[14] Hearne's calculations placed the mouth of the Coppermine in both wrong longitude and latitude. These mistakes were corrected by Franklin in 1820.

pack moved in and out constantly with wind and tide, and consisted of huge masses of ice quite unlike anything he had come up against before. Parry didn't know it but he had met the edge of the main ice stream issuing from the Arctic Ocean through the opening of M'Clure Strait. On September 17th they reached longitude 112 degrees, fifty-one minutes west, close to the coast of Melville Island. Beyond this they could not go.

Three days later the ships met near disaster. Hugging close to the shore of Melville Island Parry tried to press on along the narrow lane of water between the massive floes and the shore. Suddenly the ice began to move, to grind in towards the beach. The two ships were trapped in the ever-narrowing water channel by a massive floe with pinnacles of ice that reached up higher than the mastheads of the ships. Relentlessly the ice pushed in on the *Hecla* and *Gripper*, forcing them over on their sides, pushing them towards the land. There was nothing Parry could do to free the ships; all he could do was wait, and pray that the pressure would subside before the ship's hulls were crushed, or they were driven up on the shore and wrecked.

> . . . as nothing was now to be expected but her being driven on the beach I ordered the rudder to be lifted, the sails to be furled and the top-gallant yards to be ready for striking.[15]

The hulls of the ships creaked and groaned under the tremendous pressure of the moving ice. Both vessels were tipped far over on their beams. Lieutenant Liddon, on the *Gripper*, lay against the rail on the lee side of his heeled-over ship, so stricken with rheumatism that he could neither stand nor walk, calmly directing his men as they brought down the sails and spars onto the deck. He refused Parry's offer to be carried across to the nearby *Hecla* until the danger passed, replying that he would be the last, not the first, to leave his ship.

Just when it seemed that nothing could save the ships from destruction, Parry saw that the rubbery new ice in the channel

[15] Sir William Edward Parry, *Journal of a Voyage . . .* , p. 91.

was piling up to form a resilient bumper between the ship and the shore. His hopes rose. He felt the *Hecla* tremble slightly and settle back towards a more even keel. The pressure of the ice pack slackened off slightly. Slowly, ever so slowly, the heavy ice eased off and the ships gradually rolled back to their upright position. Open water appeared in the channel again. The two ships floated free.

Parry knew he had to get the ships free of this dangerous coast before the ice moved in again. The only safe course was to retreat along the coast until he could find a harbour in which the two ships could spend the winter in safety, ready for another try next year. Reluctantly he ordered the ships about. On September 22nd the *Hecla* and *Gripper* rounded Cape Hearne once again, and sought sanctuary in the cove under its lee. Four inches of new ice covered the waters of the sheltered inlet and a canal had to be cut for a distance of two miles, along which the ships were towed into the confines of the harbour. Officers and men alike joined in the tedious work at the saws.

> The thermometer was at 6 degrees in the morning, and only rose to 9 degrees at noon. For men to work in the water under such circumstances is very severe and trying; but our crews are composed of no common men; they do everything cheerfully and well. . . . at 3.15 on September 26th we reached our winter quarters with three loud and hearty cheers from both ships' companies.[16]

The sheltered cove into which they had cut their way with so much labour, Parry named Winter Harbour. It was here, in 1947, that the Resolute weather station and airfield was to have been established. It was here, in 1961, that the first deep drilling for oil in the High Arctic islands took place. It was at this historic spot, in 1819, that English sailors, for the first time, planned to spend a winter in the Canadian Arctic, farther west and north than anyone had ever been before.

[16] Ann Parry, *Parry of the Arctic*, p. 56.

The First Wintering

No retreat, no retreat,
they must conquer or die,
who have no retreat.

Explorers had wintered on Arctic coasts long before Parry froze in his ships at Winter Harbour in the autumn of 1819. Early in the seventeenth century Henry Hudson and Thomas James had watched men weaken and die from scurvy and cold on the shore of James Bay. Jens Munck had left sixty frozen bodies on the bank of the Churchill River. In 1719 James Knight and his men had left their bones to bleach on the barren shore of Marble Island in Hudson Bay. These had been winterings of necessity not plan, and they had left a deep scar on the minds of most men from western Europe who sailed to Arctic America seeking the elusive Northwest Passage waterway. They saw the Arctic winter as a time of "dark, dark, dark . . . without all hope of day,"[1] where "snow and rock and broken ice surrounded on every side,"[2] a dreary time when men could easily be "weary for want of occupation, for want of thought, and for want of society, where today is as yesterday, as was today, so would be tomorrow."[3]

[1] John Milton, *Samson Agonistes*.
[2] John von Payer, *New Lands Within the Arctic Circle* (London: Macmillan, 1876).
[3] Sir John Ross, *Narrative of a . . . .*

I do not think I could ever imagine a more desolate coast than this appeared to be. The land seemed to be covered with everlasting snow, and might be said to be one vast glacier, with merely the capes protruding towards the sea. It was horrible to look at, and frightful to contemplate the results of a disaster to a ship's crew thrown upon it.[4]

Sir Allen Young's description of the east coast of Ellesmere Island in the summer month of August does not describe the land about Winter Harbour on Melville Island, but it does indicate the basic feeling of most English mariners who sailed to the Canadian Arctic early in the nineteenth century. It indicates the feeling of many people to this day.

In the winter of 1819-20, at a location deep in the Arctic islands some 4,000 miles from home base in England, over 1,000 miles from the nearest fur-trade fort in northwestern Canada, and at least 300 miles away from the nearest groups of Eskimo hunters on Victoria Island, Boothia Peninsula and Baffin Island, Edward Parry gambled that he and his men could live, work, and undertake limited travel throughout a High Arctic winter. The stakes were as high as they could be. It would be at least ten months before the ships could set sail again. With no retreat, he and his men had to succeed or die.

Before sailing to the Arctic, Parry's record as a naval officer had been good but undistinguished. Except for his work in astronomy and surveying he seems to have made no great impact on the service. But in command of an Arctic expedition he came into his own. Long before the ships left England he had made careful plans for a wintering in Arctic ice and, once the *Hecla* and *Gripper* were securely frozen in at Winter Harbour, the plans were put into effect. Parry had the upper masts and yards removed from both vessels and stored on shore. By lashing the lower yards fore and aft amidships, and laying planks across,

4 Sir Allen William Young, *The Two Voyages of Pandora in 1875 and 1876* (London: Stanford, 1879), pp. 134, 135.

he built frames over which the crew stretched quilted, padded canvas that had been especially prepared for this use. The ships were thus converted into two-story dwellings, which were heated by portable ovens set up on the lower deck in each main hatchway. Pipes conducted the heat to every part of the ship. To guard against fire on board Parry posted strict regulations governing the use of any flame, and he had water holes kept open through the sea ice near the main entrances. The holes were used also to record, on a graduated pole anchored to the sea bottom, the tidal range in the bay.

As soon as there was sufficient snow Parry had both ships buried to the gunwales for extra warmth. Probably he was unaware of the excellent insulating quality of loose snow. He used it because it was the only material available locally. On shore he had his men construct a small wooden building in which Captain Sabine set up a magnetic and meteorological station, the first in the Arctic islands of Canada. Between the ships and the observatory he ran lines on pillars of snow, along which the officers, who were to take observations through the twenty-four hours of every day, could move back and forth in the worst winter storms. Before the long dark of winter set in he had poles erected on the hills about the harbour, each with an arrow on top pointing in the direction of the ships.

In mid-October the men saw the sun for the last time. For a few minutes about noon it peeked over the horizon to the south, bathing the snow-covered land in red, red light. Then it slipped below the hills and was gone. They wouldn't see it again until early February the following year. For four months they were to live and work in a world of darkness, relieved only by the blue-grey light of midday, and by the light of the aurora or the bright moon shining on the snow. The men felt little dismay.

The Officers and Ship's company danced to the Organ on deck for two hours. Nothing can look more snug and comfortable than our deck does now, with a lamp on the quarter-deck and forecastle. The Aurora Borealis was seen very faintly . . . in the S.W. quarter, and near the horizon.[5]

Discipline for the crew was strict, but sane. Parry observed that "sailors must resemble children in all those points where their own health and comfort are concerned,"[6] and he drew up a list of regulations covering all aspects of the lives of officers and crew. Officers were made responsible for the health and well-being of the men. Once each week everyone was inspected by the doctors for any sign of scurvy. To help prevent this dreaded disease, pickles and vinegar were eaten and Parry insisted that every man drink lime juice and sugar daily, in front of an officer who duly recorded the fact. Parry didn't know that freshness of vegetable, fruit or meat was the quality that would help hold scurvy at bay, and he did not understand the antiscorbutic effect of eating fresh meat. But he organized hunting parties to procure deer, rabbits and ptarmigan, all of which helped keep his men healthy, from eating the meat, and happy, from the pleasure and exercise of the hunt. All game procured was common property. Everyone had his share of the fresh meat except that the owner of the gun was allowed to keep for himself the head and heart of the kill.

So long as there were a few hours of dim light at midday the men hunted in the hills around the bay. They saw only one bear which they were unable to kill. Although wounded many times it escaped into the open water off the entrance to the harbour. Caribou were plentiful but the hunters displayed little skill in stalking in a land without trees or bushes; indeed, without cover of any kind. Handling a muzzle-loading rifle in the extreme cold was difficult, at least, as Parry remarked, "for the credit of our sportsmen, we were willing to allow."[7] Notwithstanding the signposts erected on the hills, there was danger that men would be lost in the excitement of the chase:

[5] Sir William Edward Parry, *Journal of a Voyage* . . . , p. 109.
[6] *Ibid.*, p. 105.
[7] *Ibid.*, p. 108.

A party . . . being led on by the ardour of pursuit, forgot my order that every person should be on board before sunset, and did not return till late, and after we had much apprehension on their account. I, therefore, directed that the expense of rockets and other signals made in such cases should, in future be charged against the wages of the offending party.[8]

As the long Arctic night deepened and the men became more and more confined to the ship, Parry organized regular shipboard activities in which everyone took part. An amateur theatrical group was formed with Lieutenant Beechey as manager. The first production, "Miss in her Teens" was acclaimed a sellout success. One Midshipman Ross, having a girlish complexion, was conned into taking many of the female roles. Twice a month plays were presented on the *Hecla*'s deck to the assembled companies of both ships and, when the stock of existing works was exhausted, officers wrote new ones. Parry himself co-authored a smash success operetta called "The Northwest Passage," with a cast of seven actors representing five crewmen, an Eskimo and a polar bear. At times the temperature on stage hovered well below zero. Despite their best efforts with the ovens and strategically placed heated shot, the actors were in no little danger of suffering frostbite during the performance.

Christmas came and went with much merry-making on board. In January, temperatures plunged into the minus forties and fifties. Snow fell as dry, frost-like crystals and Parry felt it was too cold to allow the men to go onshore to exercise.

They run around the decks to a tune which they whistle, or to a Greenland song, which some of the old Fishermen have been accustomed to. I verily believe there never was a more merry and cheerful set of men than ours, and I must in justice add that they seem fully sensible of attending to the precautions adopted for the preservation of their health.[9]

[8] *Ibid.*
[9] Ann Parry, *Parry of the Arctic*, p. 61.

The supply of coal on the ships was not sufficient to keep the stoves going during the "night" hours and, in the extreme cold, it proved impossible to keep the ship warm. Greatcoats and mitts had to be worn in the cabin throughout the evening while the officers read, played chess or worked on the next operetta or play. Parry spent a good deal of time practising on his violin and he worked out a paper plan for a retreat south in case of a disaster to the ships in the ice. He started a ship's newspaper with Captain Sabine as editor. *The North Georgia Gazette and Winter Chronicle*[10] was published at regular intervals throughout the winter. Anyone could contribute articles or letters for publication and, to ensure anonymity of authors, a box was placed on the *Hecla*'s capstan to which the editor of the paper held the only key. Regular contributions from all literate persons on board were ensured by having non-contributors brought up before the "Non-contributors in The Court of Common-Sense."[11]

On February 3rd, from the top of the masthead, they had their first glimpse of the returning sun peeking over the southern horizon. Each succeeding day it climbed a little higher in the midday sky. The sun brought no return of warmth. February was the coldest month with a daily mean temperature of minus thirty-two degrees Fahrenheit, and an absolute minimum of minus fifty-five. It was during this period of extreme cold that they had their first emergency. Captain Sabine's servant tried to dry his handkerchief on top of the stove in the observatory and it burst into flame which spread quickly to the walls of the tiny hut. Despite the heroic efforts of officers and men they were unable to save the building, but Sergeant Smith, the man who had started the fire, ran outside with the precious dip-needle in his bare hands, saving it from destruction. Four of his fingers were so badly frostbitten they had to be amputated. A

---

[10] Parry called the land north of Viscount Melville Sound, "North Georgia." Later the islands were named Parry Islands.

[11] Ann Parry, *Parry of the Arctic*, p. 106.

number of officers and men suffered frostbitten hands and faces as they fought the fire in the well below zero temperature.

Hours of daylight increased rapidly until, by the end of March, it was light twenty-four hours of every day. Until this time the men had remained healthy, except for one mild case of scurvy in January ("a Gunner of the *Hecla*, a spare man of temperate habits but with a constitution somewhat worn by servitude in warm climates").[12] But, late in March, several crew members began to complain of sore gums, one of the first easily recognizable symptoms of scurvy. Parry was apprehensive at this development despite the fact that he had anticipated some cases of the disease during the long winter confinement on the vessels. When the first case occurred in January he had started a small garden, in a box set alongside the heating pipe running through his cabin. Mustard and cress seeds were planted in earth brought from England for this purpose. Now he enlarged his tiny garden to produce a small quantity of fresh greens for the stricken men.

> I shall be thankfull should it prove that we can cure, or even check the disease by our own resources; for I cannot help feeling some confidence that, under Providence, our making the Northwest Passage depends upon it.[13]

As with many of his observations, Parry was correct. Fortunately the men all recovered with the strengthened diet.

April brought heavy snow, more than had fallen all the previous months of midwinter. There was so much snow that Captain Sabine, who often remained all night long in the rebuilt observatory, had to be dug out each morning. In May, with the temperatures still well below freezing most of the time, but with the sun riding around the full circumference of the sky for twenty-four hours of each cloudless day, the men began to pre-

---

[12] Sir William Edward Parry, *Journal of a Voyage* . . . , p. clxiv.
[13] Ann Parry, *Parry of the Arctic*, p. 63.

pare the ships for the sea. Working with a will at the huge saws they cut the ice from around the ships. Much to their surprise, both *Hecla* and *Gripper* rose up about eighteen inches higher out of the water—the result of loss of weight from the stores consumed during the winter. On May 25th rain fell on the decks for the first time that year. It was "a considerable curiosity and I believe every person on board hastened on deck to witness so interesting as well as so unusual a phenomenon."[14]

June 1st, 1820, was a momentous day at Winter Harbour. Parry, With Captain Sabine and nine men, started off on an overland expedition across Melville Island. (They didn't know it was an island.) This was the first time that English explorers in Arctic Canada had left their ships to extend the range of exploration by land travel. To transport their equipment and supplies they had constructed a small, wooden cart, pulled by the men themselves. On it they hauled two tents, a quantity of split firewood, a cooking outfit called a "conjuror," and enough food for three weeks on the trail. Later travellers in the Arctic, using dogs and sleds, would ridicule Parry's cart, or be amused by it, but its use marked a giant step forward for exploration in the High Arctic. The cart worked well enough to carry the supplies for some 115 miles before it collapsed.

Parry and his men travelled at night to take advantage of snow rendered hard by late evening and early morning frost. It took them a week to cross the island. Pure chance had set the direction of their march north across Melville at its narrowest point. Inland they found the land a featureless plain, and they steered by means of a compass as if on a ship at sea.

> We continued our journey to northward over the same snowy and level plain as before, than which it was impossible to conceive anything more dreary and uninteresting. It frequently happened that, for an hour together, not a single spot of uncovered ground could be seen. The few patches of

[14] Sir William Edward Parry, *Journal of a Voyage . . .* , p. 178.

this kind forcibly reminded one of the description given of the oases in the deserts of Africa, not only because they relieved us for a time from the intense glare of the sun upon the snow, which was extremely oppressive to the eyes, but it was on these alone that we were able to pitch our tents to rest, or that we could expect to meet with any water. The breeze freshened up to a gale from the SSE as we proceeded, and the men, as if determined not to forget that they were sailors, set a large blanket upon the cart as a sail, which, upon this level ground, was found to be of material assistance.[15]

When they reached the north coast, so smoothly did snow-covered land run into snow-covered sea that Parry wasn't sure he had arrived at the sea until his men chopped a hole through fourteen feet of ice and he tasted the salt of the water. He named the body of water Sabine Bay, and, after stopping for only a few hours, turned his party about and set off southwest. By this time the snow was melting. Much water ran over the flat land and down the gulleys. Travel was slow and tedious compared to the trip out. The cart collapsed and they made a huge bonfire of the remains, except for the bright red wheels which they left lying on the shore of Liddon Gulf where they were found by M'Clintock thirty years later. Carrying food and ammunition on their backs, they walked to the ships at Winter Harbour.

All through June and July Parry waited for the ice to go out and free the ships but, although the ice melted along the shore of the harbour, the *Hecla* and *Gripper* remained frozen into the central mass. On July 24th sail was raised on both ships and they were forced through a mile of rotting ice towards the harbour entrance. On the last day of July the ice across the harbour mouth moved out suddenly en masse and, on August 1st, the anniversary of the day they had arrived off the entrance to Lancaster Sound the year before, the *Hecla* and *Gripper* left Winter Harbour for the last time and set off again for the West.

They didn't get far. By the 5th they reached the point of

[15] *Ibid.*, pp. 185, 186.

farthest advance of 1819 and once again they ran up against the heavy flow of pack ice through M'Clure Strait. Doggedly Parry sought a way through. The *Gripper* had her rudder cracked against the underwater foot of a huge floe, and it was unshipped and repaired with difficulty. At a point some fifty miles west of Winter Harbour they could go no farther. On August 16th Parry and Sabine walked a few miles west along the coast and named a distant point of land Cape Dundas. From the top of a hill they thought they could see the loom of land on the horizon to the southwest.

> The extent of the land now discovered gave rise to some speculations, as to its being part of the continent of America. . . . This land . . . which is the Western most land yet discovered in the Polar Sea . . . was honoured with the name of Bank's Land, after the Right Honble. Sir Joseph Banks, the venerable and worthy President of the Royal Society.[16]

Today it is called Banks Island, the westernmost island of the Canadian Arctic Archipelago.

Parry had no choice but to turn back east and run along the northern edge of the ice stream, searching for an opening through which he might sail south and look for a passage at a lower latitude. By this time he recognized that the ice he had met in M'Clure Strait was unusual.

> It now became evident, from the combined experience of this and the preceding year, that there was something peculiar about the southwest extremity of Melville Island, which made the icy sea there extremely unfavourable to navigation, and which seemed likely to bid defiance to all our efforts to proceed much further to the westward in this parallel of latitude.[17]

His experience with the pack ice issuing from the Arctic Ocean

[16] Ann Parry, *Parry of the Arctic*, p. 238.
[17] *Ibid.*

through M'Clure Strait brought him to advocate finding a passage through the more southerly entrance of Hudson Strait. By doing this Parry turned immediate future exploration for the Northwest Passage away from the route he pioneered into the dead end (for all practical purposes) of Foxe Basin and Hudson Bay. It was one of the few mistakes Parry ever was to make in his Arctic explorations.

From Melville Sound east to Lancaster Sound Parry found solid ice blocking all openings to the south. He decided to return to England and report on his partial success. His ships were provisioned for only a two-year stay in the Arctic and he could not risk another wintering. On the return trip he sailed south through Baffin Bay and surveyed the northeast coast of Baffin Island as far south as latitude sixty-eight degrees. On September 27th, his ships bore away for England. On the 31st of October, 1820, the *Hecla* limped into the port of Peterhead after being badly battered by a north Atlantic storm. The *Gripper* arrived at the Shetland Islands the following day. This most successful of all Arctic voyages to that date had ended. Parry brought his two ships and ninety-four men home to England with the loss of only one man.

Parry made three more trips to the Arctic region but only two of them to North American waters. The summer following his return from Lancaster Sound he sailed through Hudson Strait and Foxe Basin, in the ships *Hecla* and *Fury*, testing his theory that the Passage should be sought at a lower latitude than Lancaster Sound. He froze the ships in at Winter Island, off the southern coast of Melville Peninsula. There he and his men met Eskimo hunters for the first time. As soon as the ships were released from the ice in the summer of 1822, Parry pushed north along the east coast of Melville Peninsula, to winter a second time at Igloolik Island. From there he discovered the strait between the peninsula and Baffin Island, naming it after his two ships. Unable to sail through the strait he returned to England in the summer of 1823.

In 1824 he was back in the Arctic again, once more with the

Hecla and *Fury*, this time entering through Lancaster Sound. He sailed south down Prince Regent Inlet, hoping to reach open water at the western end of Fury and Hecla Strait, from which point he thought he could sail along the north mainland coast to the Pacific. But this time his luck ran out. He was forced to winter on the west coast of Brodeur Peninsula at Port Bowen and, in the summer of 1825 when he tried to sail south again, the *Fury* was driven ashore and wrecked on Somerset Island at what is now Fury Point. The crew was saved and everyone returned to England on board the *Hecla*.

In the summer of 1827 Parry changed the direction of his thrust into the north and attempted to lead a party of men to the true North Pole over the sea ice north of Spitsbergen. Despite tremendous effort he and his men were unable to make headway across ice that was constantly drifting south, away from the Arctic Ocean, and the attempt had to be abandoned. But they had set a record for the farthest northern exploration that stood for nearly fifty years. This trip ended Parry's Arctic explorations. He was appointed Admiralty Hydrographer in 1827 and, two years later, he was knighted by the Queen and awarded an honorary degree by the University of Oxford.

In 1829 Parry accepted the post of commissioner at the Australian Agricultural Company in New South Wales. He and his wife Isabella and four children spent about four years at Port Stephens, ninety miles north of Sydney, where his great organizational ability brought a measure of good management and good government to the budding agricultural colony. But ill health forced him to return to England where, in 1835, he was appointed Assistant Poor-Law Commissioner in Norfolk. The work proved to be too heavy for him and he resigned from this post one year later. In 1837 he was appointed head of a new department at the Admiralty as Controller of Steam Machinery and, in 1841, he was given the task of supervising the building of the Caledonian Canal in the Highlands of Scotland. He presided at its opening in April 1847.

For the next six years Parry was Captain Superintendent at

the Naval Hospital at Haslar, Gosport. During this time he gave advice on the naval searches for his close friend, John Franklin, missing in the Arctic since 1845. In 1854 a cholera epidemic struck parts of London and Parry was advised to travel abroad to consult doctors about his rapidly deteriorating health. The trip was to no avail. On July 8th, 1855 he died at Ems, Germany. His body was brought home to England and interred at Greenwich.

His famous ship *Hecla*, which had carried him safely through four successive voyages into the Arctic ice, also retired from Arctic service following the last voyage north in 1827. Although Parry protested vigorously, the *Hecla* was sent to survey the warm ocean waters off the coast of Africa. From this part of the world her new captain wrote to Parry on the day the *Hecla* crossed the equator. Nothing is known of the ultimate fate of this stout ship which carried one of England's foremost ice navigators on his epic voyages into the far north.

Edward Parry's main claim to fame came from his discovery of new lands and new sea channels across Arctic America. But his major success lay in proving that men could overwinter in the Arctic without fear of death from starvation, cold or scurvy, providing they were properly provisioned and properly supervised. Parry was the first in a long line of innovators in the Arctic—M'Clintock, Rae, Sverdrup, Stefansson—each of whom built on the solid foundation established by Parry in the winter of 1819-20. The modern Arctic explorer, Vilhjalmur Stefansson, a great man and a personal favourite I was fortunate enough to meet on a number of occasions before his death in 1962 at the age of eighty-two, was critical of Parry because he felt the explorer had relied too much on lime juice and amateur theatricals to keep his men healthy and happy during the long winter nights. Stefansson felt that Parry should have realized the value of hunting as a full-time winter occupation, and the value of fresh meat as the major food to combat scurvy in the Arctic. Stefansson was right—in hindsight. But all innovation must have a starting point and, this usually falls far short of the ideal. Parry's achievements and methods were not perfect, but they were great for his time. In one trip to the Arctic he almost discovered the Northwest Passage and, at a time when most men were as afraid of Arctic winters as they were of the fires of hell, he proved that men could winter safely in the high north.

Who Was John Franklin?

Ghosts haunt the ice-covered sea lanes off the north coast of America and the shores of the islands scattered around the rim of the Arctic sea: ghosts of fine ships left to be crushed and torn by the polar pack, ghosts of Arctic wanderers who drifted into oblivion leaving almost no mark that they once passed that way, ghosts of men from western Europe who were abandoned or who disappeared in the white wilderness of the Arctic land. The ghost of Parry's ship, *Fury*, sails easily through the ice-choked waters of Prince Regent Inlet. The shadow of M'Clure's *Investigator* drifts slowly through Viscount Melville Sound. Images of the men and women of the "lost" Greenland colony haunt the coves of Baffin Island. Henry Hudson's spirit hangs over Charlton Island in James Bay. James Knight walks the lonely beaches of Marble Island in Hudson Bay. Ghosts of murdered Eskimos hang in the air above Bloody Falls on the Coppermine. The spirits of Jens Munck's sailors drift about the walls of Fort Prince of Wales. Shades of Martin Frobisher's five seamen sail forever over the waters of the bay they thought would lead them to Cathay.

But of all the ghosts of men and ships that pervade the land and sea of Arctic Canada none are as powerful as those that linger along the bleak shores of King William Island and Adelaide Peninsula, the ghosts of the ships *Erebus* and *Terror*, and of the 126 officers and men of the British Navy who manned them.[1] Their leader was Sir John Franklin. Men still travel north to search for his last resting place. His name is familiar to most Canadians for it is dotted across our maps— Fort Franklin, Franklin Bay, Franklin Strait, Franklin Lake, Franklin Point, District of Franklin, and, at the bottom of my street in the city of Yellowknife, the Sir John Franklin School. Almost every schoolboy knows the story of his disappearance in Arctic Canada. Almost every historian and author lauds his abilities and his achievements. He was held in high esteem by most of his contemporary explorers, knighted by his Queen, given an honorary degree by the University of Oxford. His close friend Sir Edward Parry once said, in response to a remark that John Franklin had a fine head: "Yes, indeed; it is the finest I know; inside as well as out."

Yet when I write about John Franklin, I am troubled. Words stick on the point of my pen. I wrote about Frobisher and Hearne and Parry and the words flowed. I write about Franklin and the words come slowly, reluctantly. On the one hand I admire his major successes in exploration, as well as his perseverance, his great courage in the face of death and danger. On the other hand I cannot forget that of the three expeditions he led into the North American Arctic, the first ended in near total tragedy with deaths from starvation, cold, murder and execution, and the third ended in complete tragedy—two ships lost and 129 dead, including Sir John Franklin himself. I know most of the reasons why Franklin's two expeditions suffered such misfortune. Taken individually they were things over which he had little personal control. I can find a dozen excuses for his difficulties, for the deaths of his men and himself. But the doubt

[1] The references to the number of Franklin's men vary from time to time. When he started out on his third expedition there were 129 in all. Three died at Beechey Island during the first wintering. One hundred and five started down the coast on the march. One hundred and forty is the total number of men lost on the two tragic expeditions.

remains. Was John Franklin really as great as many believed him to be? What is it that has brought his name to figure so prominently in the history of our Arctic? Whom do we honour on our maps—Franklin the man, or Franklin the ghost?

John Franklin was born on April 15th, 1786, at Spilsby, Lincolnshire. His father was a shopkeeper in the town. Very early in life he decided that he would become a sailor and, when he was fourteen years of age, his father was able to send him to sea on a merchant ship bound for Lisbon. On his return from this voyage he joined the British Navy as a First Class Volunteer on the *H.M.S. Polyphemus*. One year later he transferred to the *Investigator* and sailed on that ship to Australia and the Antarctic. Franklin's life as an explorer began when he was only fifteen years old.

In 1803, at age seventeen, Franklin joined the *Porpoise* and was on board that vessel when it, and a companion ship *Cato*, both struck a reef en route from Sydney to London. The vessels foundered and the survivors of the wrecks, young Franklin amongst them, managed to make their way to shore on the barren reef, a tiny oasis of rock about 150 feet long and ninety feet wide. A third ship, *Bridgewater*, which was travelling with the *Porpoise* and *Cato*, sailed off to Bombay to report the two ships lost with all hands. No rescue attempt seemed necessary. By good fortune the survivors had managed to salvage one of their ship's small boats and in it two officers and twelve men made the 750-mile trip to Sydney to advise of the survivors' plight. They had a relief expedition sent back for the people still stranded on the desolate reef. As with Martin Frobisher and Samuel Hearne, Franklin's early days at sea were anything but easy.

In 1805 Franklin was serving on board the *H.M.S. Bellerephon*[2] when that ship took part in the famous battle of Trafalgar. The *Bellerephon* engaged the French ship *Aigle* and the two raked each other with murderous, close-in fire from banked

[2] This was the ship on which Napoleon, defeated at Waterloo, was carried to Plymouth and then exiled on St. Helena.

cannons. A second French warship also blazed away at the *Bellerephon* from the opposite side. The French ships were the first to withdraw, but 300 of Franklin's fellow sailors were dead or wounded in the engagement. Franklin himself escaped serious injury but forever afterwards he suffered from deafness brought on by the terrific cannonade.

By 1812 Franklin had risen to the rank of Lieutenant and was serving on board the *Bedford* when that ship was sent to take part in the expedition against the port of New Orleans. At the end of the War of 1812 Franklin found himself faced with the same prospects as Edward Parry, that of half-pay officer in the Navy, with few places to go and no one left to fight.

John Franklin first met Edward Parry in the naval shipyard at Deptford in 1818, the year in which Parry was to sail to Baffin Bay as second in command to John Ross, and Franklin was to sail to the north of Spitsbergen as second in command to Captain Buchan. The two became fast friends. Their lives would be linked in almost every Arctic endeavour to take place over the next twenty-five years. In 1819, when Parry was named to command his famous first expedition to Lancaster Sound, Franklin was despatched on a companion expedition. He was sent to explore and map the unknown north coast of America by travelling through Hudson Bay, along the Hayes, Saskatchewan and Athabasca rivers, to reach Great Slave Lake. From there he was to make his way to the north coast at the mouth of the Coppermine River. This had not been visited since Samuel Hearne's expedition of fifty years before, and was still the only part of the central north coast to have been visited by an explorer.[3] From the mouth of the Coppermine, Franklin was to map the unknown coast to the east, and to make contact with Parry should Parry be successful in his attempt to sail the *Hecla* and *Gripper* through the Northwest Passage.

[3] Alexander Mackenzie had reached the Arctic Ocean at the mouth of the river named after him in 1786. These were the only two known points on the coast between Repulse Bay in the east and Point Barrow in the west.

Unlike Parry's voyage to Lancaster Sound, Franklin's trip to the north coast very nearly ended in total disaster. Franklin depended on the good offices of the Hudson's Bay Company and the Northwest Company to provide him with transport to Great Slave Lake, as well as with canoes, canoemen, stores and provisions for his trip along the north coast and for his advance base, wherever that might be set up in the northern bush. But, in 1819, the great fur-trade war between the two companies was at its climax. Men from both companies were engaged in a relentless struggle for supremacy on the rivers of western and northwestern Canada. They had little time for British Navy explorers, tenderfeet at northern bush travel, who would only place additional supply burdens on their beleaguered posts. Despite the letters assuring cooperation from the principal officers of both companies, Franklin ran into a great deal of trouble in procuring adequate transport and sufficient supplies for his expedition. And few people in the northwest seemed to care a whit about the expedition. This disregard contributed much to the troubles experienced by the expedition, particularly on its return journey from the coast.

It took Franklin a year to reach Great Slave Lake, and another to build an advance base at a location near Point Lake which he called Fort Enterprise. Not until the summer of 1822 was he able to reach the north coast at the mouth of the Coppermine (guided by an Indian chief named Akaitcho) and begin his survey of the coast to the east.[4] By this time Parry had completed his first voyage to Lancaster Sound, and had sailed to Hudson Strait on his second voyage in the *Fury* and *Hecla*. With a party of nineteen men—Dr. John Richardson, Midshipmen George Back and Robert Hood, Seaman John Hepburn, and fifteen Canadian voyageurs and interpreters—Franklin paddled slowly east in two huge canoes, hoping to reach Repulse Bay

[4] He visited the falls on the Coppermine, saw the bones of the Eskimos massacred by Hearne's Indians, and named the location Bloody Falls.

and complete a survey of the entire length of the unknown north central coast.

His objective was impossible, but he couldn't have known that. By superhuman effort he managed to survey over 500 miles of coast before dwindling supplies and storms of the onrushing autumn forced him to turn back. Despite the mileage accomplished he had made little progress towards Repulse Bay. He became entangled in the labyrinth of channels that dips deep into the north coast at Bathurst Inlet, and also in the deep bay to the south of Kent Peninsula. Late August found him on the northwest coast of Kent Peninsula. At a place he called Turnagain Point he decided to turn back, and on August 22nd, 1822 Franklin started for the base at Fort Enterprise. On the same day, some 600 miles to the east at Winter Island in Foxe Basin, quite unknown to Franklin, Edward Parry took his ships out of their winter harbour and started north for Igloolik.

In the event of failure to reach Repulse Bay Franklin had planned to retreat along the coast the way he had come.[5] But the lateness of the season, the great waves from fall storms that crashed on the open south shore of Coronation Gulf, and the dearth of game found along this coast on the way out, made him change his mind. He decided to return overland. He took his party south into Bathurst Inlet and up the Hood River as far as they could go in the canoes. Then they left the river, broke up the big canoes to make two smaller ones that could be carried, and set off on foot towards their base, over 200 miles away. The only maps of the country towards which they were headed were the simple charts of Samuel Hearne.

The story of this trek across the tundra and northern bush to Fort Enterprise is one of toil, hardship and slow starvation. The voyageurs carried ninety-pound packs and the two canoes. The

[5] Arrangements had been made with the Hudson's Bay Company for a supply depot to be established on the west coast of Hudson Bay, to be used by Franklin if he got that far.

officers carried "as much as they were capable of."[6] The tundra soil was full of sharp stones which cut their moccasins and boots. In the high winds that swept across the open tundra the voyageurs found it very difficult and tiring carrying the canoes. At the end of the first week in September they experienced the first blizzard of the year which left them shivering in their tents surrounded by three-foot snow drifts. Day after day they saw only the odd caribou. They ate the last of their supply of pemmican and had to resort to eating tripe de roche, a barely edible lichen scraped from the rocks. One of the canoes was smashed when blown onto a rock, and they chopped it up for firewood and pressed on.

On September 9th they came to the shore of a large lake which stretched far to the west and flowed out through a wide river. Here they made a serious mistake, brought about by the wrong latitudes and longitudes marked on Hearne's charts. Using the remaining canoe they crossed the river and in so doing put themselves inside the huge water triangle formed by Contwoyto and Kathawachaga lakes, both of which now lay between themselves and their goal. If they had not crossed the river at this point but had made only a minor detour to the north and west they would have had almost clear walking home. As it was it took them almost a week to extricate themselves from the dead end into which they had unwittingly gone.

They killed two caribou which helped to relieve the hunger pangs for a few days but, crossing a wide river, the canoe with Franklin and two voyageurs on board, swamped in a rapid. All three men were pitched into the icy, rushing water. Fortunately it came only up to their waists and they managed to save the canoe. Standing in the river they bailed it free of water, but only Franklin and one voyageur had the strength left to climb on board. Franklin helped paddle the canoe to shore and the

---

[6] Sir John Franklin, *Narrative of a Journey to the Shores of the Polar Sea in the years 1819-20-21-22* (New York: J. M. Dent and Sons Ltd. and E. P. Dutton and Co.).

stranded voyageur was dragged across by a rope. He was unconscious, and only after being bundled into a sleeping robe with a man on either side for a few hours did he come round and regain the use of his legs.

On the 26th of September they reached the east bank of the Coppermine River at a point only a few days journey from Fort Enterprise. Two feet of snow covered the land but the river was still open. The last canoe had been smashed and they had no way of crossing the rushing river. For the past ten days they had lived on tripe de roche and fried deer skin. Everyone was in very bad shape. The discipline of the party began to break down. The voyageurs were tough and hardy but they were also highly emotional and fatalistic. They lacked the controlled discipline of the close-knit Navy group. Fortunately, at this critical point, they were able to kill five caribou and this revived everyone, including the voyageurs.

They still had to get across the river. Logs large enough for a raft could not be found so they built a small platform of willows, big enough to transport their supplies and themselves to the other side. But first they had to get one man with a rope across. Dr. Richardson, surgeon of the expedition and later leader of Arctic expeditions of his own, volunteered to make the attempt. Into the ice cold water he plunged and struck out for the far shore. After a few minutes his arms were numb and he couldn't swim. He floated on his back and tried to propel himself across by kicking with his legs. But, when only a short distance from the other side, he lost all feeling in his body and floated, helpless. The others dragged him back, nearly dead from exposure. It took several hours to thaw him out sufficiently to enable him to move about again. Later he would write of this episode.

It may be worthy of remark that I should have had little hesitation in any former period of my life, at plunging into water even below 38 F; but at this time I was reduced to almost skin and bone, and, like the rest of the party, suffered from degrees of cold that would have been disregarded in health and vigour.[7]

It took them eight days to get across the Coppermine. Using willows and the canvas covers of the sleeping rolls, one of the voyageurs fashioned a small canoe in which they managed to transfer themselves and their gear to the opposite bank. They were only forty miles from Fort Enterprise where they expected to find warmth and food. But several of the men were very weak, and were unable to gain enough nourishment from the tripe de roche. Franklin sent George Back with three voyageurs on ahead. They were to get provisions from the fort and bring them back, or to send Indians with help. Back and his men left while Franklin and the remainder of the party struggled on in their wake.

It was a grim race with death, and some didn't make it to the finish. Up to this point Franklin had managed to keep his group together, but now it began to fall apart as men grew weaker in varying degrees. Hood lost strength rapidly and had to be assisted by Dr. Richardson, even though the doctor himself was still partially paralysed from his swim in the river. Some of the voyageurs, who had been weakened by the loads they had carried and by their efforts at hunting, began to drop behind. Many could not digest the tripe de roche. The slightly stronger helped the weaker, waiting for them to come up if they fell behind, going back for them if they didn't appear at the stops. Three voyageurs dropped by the way and could not be found in the drifting snow. Finally Hood could go no further. Richardson remained with his patient and Hepburn volunteered to stay with them. Forever after Franklin would be grateful to Hepburn for this unselfish act.

Once again Franklin and the remainder of the party started off but, after going only a few miles, four of the voyageurs had to turn back. Only one ever reached the tent where Hood,

[7] *Ibid.*

Richardson and Hepburn awaited rescue or death. Of the nineteen men who had started out along the north coast with Franklin only five remained with their leader, and these struggled valiantly on. It took them three days to get to Fort Enterprise. As they rounded the last turn in the river each one looked eagerly for the first sight of smoke rising from the chimney. Here they expected shelter, food and rest. But the fort was empty—no fires, no food, no people. They could hardly believe their eyes. Inside the empty fort they found a short note from Back to say that he had gone to look for Indians who should be somewhere in the vicinity.

Dispirited but not yet beaten, they shovelled the loose snow out of the fort, boarded up the windows and started a fire. They found a number of deer skins under the snow outside and ate them. With the temperature hovering near twenty below zero Franklin felt they could not afford to remain at the fort and hope for assistance. Their only chance for survival was to travel south to Fort Providence on the north shore of Great Slave Lake, the nearest trading post of the Northwest Company. Franklin packed his journals in a tin box and left them with two of the voyageurs who were too weak to go farther. He gave them instructions to deliver the journals to Fort Providence in the event that he failed to last out the trip. Then, with the three remaining voyageurs, he set off for the south.

They didn't get far. The second day out Franklin broke one of his snowshoes and they had to make their slow way back to the fort. There they settled down to wait, for rescue or death.

Before either came, Richardson and Hepburn stumbled into the fort with a tale of horror to eclipse anything that had yet happened. Hood was dead, shot by a voyageur after a quarrel, as surmised by Richardson and Hepburn, although the voyageur claimed that Hood had killed himself accidentally or committed suicide. As the three men had settled down to wait for rescue following Hood's death, the voyageur had made suspicious trips into the bush nearby. He always took his axe, and brought back meat that he claimed came from a wolf killed by a deer's horns. But Richardson and Hepburn began to suspect that the meat came from the body of one of the missing voyageurs. Both men feared for their lives, particularly after the voyageur made remarks that showed them he knew they suspected him of murder and cannibalism. At the first chance Richardson and Hepburn talked over their situation and came to the conclusion the only way out was to kill the voyageur before he could kill them. Richardson volunteered, and shot the man through the head with his pistol as he returned to the camp. The voyageur was a man whom Franklin, only three weeks before, had proposed giving special reward as he was the best and most willing of all the workers.

In the fort at Enterprise the men awaited whatever the future might bring. Daily they became weaker. Somewhere in the bush to the southwest they hoped that George Back still sought the local Indians. They could only pray that he would succeed, for without their help they were lost. Unknown to them, Back, with an effort of will almost impossible to imagine, kept himself and his three men on the move, searching for tracks that would lead them to an Indian camp. The constant picture of his dying companions drove him steadily on. One of his voyageurs froze to death in the snow. Finally, on November 3rd, he came upon the tracks of Indians and followed them to the camp of their leader, Akaitcho. Within the hour Akaitcho had two sleds loaded with deer meat on the trail to Fort Enterprise. They reached there on November 8th to find only Franklin, Richardson, Hepburn and three voyageurs still alive. Of the twenty men who started out from the mouth of the Coppermine River only nine survived.

After they had recovered sufficiently to leave Fort Enterprise, Franklin and his party journeyed to Fort Providence. There Akaitcho and his family came to visit and to collect goods that Franklin had promised them for guiding him to the north coast in the early summer of that year. But due to the trade war the goods had not arrived. Akaitcho was disappointed but not dismayed.

> The world goes badly, [he said]. All are poor; you are poor, the traders appear to be poor, I and my party are poor likewise; and since the goods have not come in, we cannot have them. I do not regret having supplied you with provisions, for a Copper Indian can never permit white men to suffer from want of food in his lands, without flying to their aid. I trust, however, that we shall, as you say, receive what is due next autumn; and, at all events, it is the first time that the white people have been indebted to the Copper Indians.[8]

Franklin arrived back in England in October 1822. He was promoted to post Captain by the Admiralty and elected to a fellowship in the Royal Society. He had become as famous as his friend Parry. Everywhere in England he was lauded for his great achievement in filling in the outline of part of the previously unknown north central coast of North America. There were a few voices raised in protest over the loss of life. Some thought it odd that the dead, with one exception, were voyageurs. A few questioned the killing of the voyageur by Richardson. And, in North America, George Simpson of the Hudson's Bay Company (who had met Franklin when he was on his way north to the coast) remarked in his journal that, in his opinion, Franklin was quite unsuited to travel in the northern bush. He was unable to walk more than ten miles a day and was unwilling to forgo the pleasure of his afternoon tea. But these voices were in the minority; the legend of John Franklin had begun.

[8] *Ibid.* The goods did come in and Akaitcho received payment for services rendered.

The Mystery of Rae Strait

John Franklin returned to the Arctic coast in 1826, this time as leader of a two-pronged expedition. One section, under Franklin, travelled west from the mouth of the Mackenzie River to map the unknown coast in the direction of Point Barrow. The other, under Dr. Richardson, travelled east to map from the Mackenzie to the mouth of the Coppermine. Richardson completed his section of the survey and returned overland to the base at Fort Franklin on Great Bear Lake. Franklin nearly came to grief just as his survey was starting when he met a large group of mischievous, thieving, and potentially dangerous Eskimos in the Mackenzie Delta. But he managed to get away before major trouble developed, and surveyed west to within 150 miles of Point Barrow before ice and the lateness of the season forced him to turn back. There was no trouble with provisions on this expedition. The fur-trade war was over and Franklin had engaged Peter Warren Dease of the Hudson's Bay Company as officer in charge of provisioning and procuring, a job he undertook with great zeal.

In 1829 Franklin was knighted in a dual ceremony with Edward Parry. Both men were rewarded for their fine accomplishments in adding much new knowledge about the coastlines of Arctic America to the maps of the day.

Between them they had charted the coast along two-thirds of the elusive Northwest Passage waterway. Neither had discovered a passage but, largely as a result of their combined efforts, it was now certain one did exist. It was felt that it would be only a matter of time before a ship sailed along its length.

Following his second expedition to the Arctic coast the Admiralty posted Franklin to the Mediterranean. In 1837 he was appointed Lieutenant-Governor of Van Dieman's Land (Tasmania). As with Parry in Australia, Franklin accomplished a great deal in Tasmania. He established what was to become the Royal Society of Tasmania and did much to improve the living and working conditions of the convicts on the island. He contributed £500 towards the establishment of a university, and Lady Franklin, the former Jane Griffin whom he had married in 1828, donated 400 acres of land and a museum for the use of the proposed university.

Despite his accomplishments Franklin's tour of duty on Tasmania was not a success. He became involved in disputes with his colonial secretary in the course of which Franklin came off second best. One of the difficulties was purported to be interference in government affairs by Lady Franklin. The end result was that Franklin was dismissed from his post by the Colonial Office in London in such a way that he did not know of the dismissal until his replacement arrived on the boat in 1843. He and his wife were forced to return to England, full of resentment at the treatment afforded Franklin by the government. Much of the "right" in this affair seems to have been on Franklin's side. There is little doubt that he was treated shabbily. However, he had been a leader, and it was his leadership that came into question, not his personal capabilities in other directions.

During the time Franklin was in the Mediterranean and Tasmania, search for the Northwest Passage continued. A privately sponsored expedition to Boothia Peninsula set out under the command of John Ross. An Admiralty expedition under Captain George Back to the mouth of the Back River at Chantrey

Inlet on the north central coast started out as an expedition to search for John Ross, but became one of pure exploration when Ross turned up safe and sound. A second Admiralty expedition set out, again under Back, but although it explored Hudson Strait and Foxe Channel, it accomplished little. An expedition sponsored by the Hudson's Bay Company, under the command of Peter Dease explored the last remaining unknown sections of the coast west to Point Barrow and east to Chantrey Inlet.

As a result of these journeys almost the entire north coast of North America had been charted. Only one tiny section remained unknown: no one had yet travelled the few miles along the west coast of lower Boothia Peninsula to establish that Rae Strait existed and that King William "Land" was really an island. In 1845 the charts of this sector of the coast showed that James Ross Strait ended in an enclosed bay, which made Victoria Strait the only water channel through which ships could sail from Peel Sound and Franklin Strait to Queen Maud Gulf and the Pacific Ocean, along the north coast of the mainland. This error was to help spell death for John Franklin and 105 of his men. By a strange irony of fate, it was one of Franklin's numerous young friends and admirers in the British Navy, James Clark Ross, who began the chain of events that was to contribute so much to this greatest of all Arctic tragedies.

James Clark Ross had sailed with Edward Parry on all his Arctic voyages, including the last one, the attempt at the true North Pole over the ice north of Spitsbergen. In 1829 he sailed north again, this time on the *Victory*, a steam-paddle yacht purchased and provisioned by the London liquor magnate, Felix Booth. Ross' uncle, John Ross, was in command. The *Victory* sailed through Lancaster Sound, down Prince Regent Inlet and wintered on the east coast of Boothia Peninsula. Three years later it would be abandoned. The crew escaped by ship's boat to Lancaster Sound and by whaler to England. J. C. Ross spent the winter of 1829-30 on board the frozen-in ship at Felix Harbour waiting for the light and better weather of spring. Then he planned to explore by sled the unknown western coast of Boothia and the sea beyond for a possible Northwest Passage waterway.

He left the *Victory* late in April with six men and two sleds, one pulled by Eskimo dogs. They crossed the narrow neck of land at the base of Boothia Peninsula and came down onto sea ice near the present settlement of Spence Bay. The weather was excellent but the cold air was full of ice crystals and Ross had great difficulty perceiving detail on the unknown coast he was exploring.

> When all is ice, and all one dazzling mass of white, when the surface of the sea itself is tossed and fixed into rocks, while the land is on the contrary, often very flat, if not level . . . it is not always so easy a problem [to see].[1]

Arctic hunters and desert nomads, sailors and explorers, prairie farmers and coast fishermen all know the difficulty of "seeing" across the great open spaces of the world's surface. Refraction and reflection, mirage and distortion, blackout and white-out,[2] even preconceived notions of what "should" be seen, can make a mockery of man's sense of sight. He can see, yet he cannot see clearly. The harder he tries to see clearly, the more his sense of sight fails him. He sees land where no land exists. He sees water where no water flows. He sees mountains as water and horizons of water as ranges of rugged hills. When the air is full of fog, snow, heavy rain or ice crystals, man has great difficulty seeing anything at all.

In 1616 William Baffin saw the waterways of Smith, Jones and Lancaster sounds as enclosed bays, as did John Ross some 200 years later. Martin Frobisher saw his bay as a strait. John Davis thought enclosed Cumberland Sound would lead through to

[1] Sir John Ross, *Narrative of a Second Voyage* . . . .
[2] An Arctic weather condition that severely reduces the ability to see objects in perspective

the West. In the north Atlantic an early ship's captain called James Leech[3] saw the "Isle of Busse," which future navigators were unable to find. In the Arctic Ocean off northern Ellesmere Island, Robert Peary[4] saw "Crocker Land" where later travellers could find only mile after mile of broken sea ice. In the great open spaces of the world no mistake is easier to make than that of seeing what is not there, or of failing to see reality. In most cases such errors are corrected in due time and the original mistake does no one much harm. But every once in a while, an error in seeing contributes to unforgettable tragedy.

James Clark Ross made his way northwest across the strait named after him, and followed the west coast of King William Island south to a deep bay, now called Collinson Inlet. The point of land on which he stood before turning back he named Victory Point. From it he could see two headlands on either side of Collinson Inlet. One he named Cape Jane Franklin, and the other, Franklin Point. It was an act of grim irony that Ross should have chosen these two names, sixteen years before John Franklin was to die on board his ship, frozen into the ice within sight of the two headlands named for him and his charming, ambitious wife.

On the return journey Ross' food supply ran low but he made a detour south of Matty Island in order to try to see more clearly what lay in that direction. Standing on the low shore of one of the small islands he looked south and, through "a thin haze which covered the land,"[5] he saw Cape Colville on Boothia Peninsula reaching west. It seemed to join with the higher Mount Matheson on the King William "Land" shore. On his charts he made James Ross Strait an enclosed bay joining King William "Land" to Boothia Peninsula by a narrow isthmus where, in reality, lay the ice-covered water of Rae Strait.

[3] He was the master of the *Busse of Bridgewater*, one of Frobisher's vessels on his third voyage.
[4] Robert Peary, later Admiral Peary, was the first man to reach the true North Pole, on April 6, 1909.
[5] Sir John Ross, *Narrative of a Second Voyage* . . . .

With this error of sight Ross initiated the chain of events that would lead to the great dramatic tragedy in which his friend and mentor, John Franklin, would play the lead role, a drama the final act of which has not yet been played out in the history of Arctic Canada.

It was four years later that the next explorer came to this area of the north coast. In 1834 George Back travelled down the great river named after him to Chantrey Inlet and sailed his small boat north to Ogle Point. He tried to work west, to complete the survey of the coast as far as Point Turnagain (which had been reached from the west by himself and John Franklin in 1821), but solid ice blocked the way. To the north of Chantrey Inlet, in the direction of Rae Strait, the water was open. But Back, although he spent three weeks trying to get through the ice to the west, failed to exploit this fact. His orders were to sail west. Thus the first opportunity to correct Ross' mistake on the charts and establish the fact of an open waterway between King William "Land" and Boothia Peninsula was missed.

Five more years passed before Thomas Simpson of the Hudson's Bay Company explored the north coast from the mouth of the Coppermine to east of Chantrey Inlet. In 1838 he crossed from Cape Britannia to King William Island by small boat, passing directly along the mouth of the southern entrance to Rae Strait. But the weather was foul. Poor visibility prevented him from seeing far and he, too, failed to notice that King William "Land" was an island, and that an open water strait led off to the north. On his return south Simpson requested permission from his uncle to complete the exploration east from Chantrey Inlet, but Governor Simpson refused. The younger Simpson then transferred his request to the Governors of the Company in London, who granted it. But before word of this could reach Thomas Simpson at Red River he became impatient at the delay (he was a very impatient and impetuous young man), and left for New York intending to travel overland to catch a ship for England. On the way he either committed suicide or was murdered after killing one of his Métis companions. Thus his trip to the north coast never took place and the last chance to correct the error on the charts was lost. The next expedition to come to this sector of the north coast was that commanded by Sir John Franklin.

Journey to
King William Island

Cambridge Bay Airport, southern Victoria Island, April 1962. I sat in the narrow front seat of my Super Cub watching the gauges on the panel jump and flutter in response to the start of the Lycoming engine in the minus thirty degree temperature of the bitter Arctic morning. Reluctantly the oil pressure needle popped free from its peg and started to climb slowly. For fifteen minutes I let the engine warm up, then, with a quick burst of power to free the skis from the grip of hard snow, I taxied out towards the smooth snow strip alongside the gravel runway at this windswept Arctic airfield.

For the past month I had been on the move, the plane loaded with cameras, recorders and emergency gear. West across Canada from Ottawa via Kapuskasing, Kenora, Dauphin, and Buffalo Narrows to McMurray on the Athabasca shore; then north to Fort Smith and Yellowknife; west to Fort Simpson and northwest to Aklavik and Inuvik down the Mackenzie River. From Inuvik I had flown northeast to Cape Parry, then east, high above the western channels of the Northwest Passage waterway, to Cambridge Bay. Ahead lay another four weeks of travel, to Spence Bay, Pelly Bay, Repulse Bay, Rankin Inlet and Churchill, before starting on the long flight south and east to home, where I was to edit the film and sound material gathered on the trip into a television program about people in the Northwest Territories.

Pre-flight and radio check, a quick look about, and I opened the throttle wide. The heavily laden plane started slowly then picked up speed. The tail came up and, in a few seconds, a light thump signified that the skis had lifted clear of the snow. Eight hundred feet above ground I banked the plane left in a wide circle to head due east, climbing steadily over the snow-covered tundra of southern Victoria Island. Half an hour later the plane passed over the low coast. Once more I flew swiftly and easily along the Northwest Passage airway.

One hour out of Cambridge Bay the DEW Line station on Jenny Lind Island passed beneath and I reported all well. In the clear air ahead the jagged outline of the Royal Geographical Society Islands broke the smooth snow surface of Markham Strait and, barely visible beyond, the low, indistinct west coast of King William Island blurred the horizon. I felt a slight tingle of excitement flutter deep inside as I looked northeast up the long reach of ice-covered Victoria Strait, and ahead to Simpson Strait between King William Island and Adelaide Peninsula. This is historic ground in Arctic Canada, forever haunted by the ghosts of Sir John Franklin, his officers and his men.

In two fine ships, the *Erebus* and *Terror,* manned by especially selected crews and well-trained officers, many of them veterans of previous Arctic voyages, Franklin sailed from England on May 19th, 1845. This was to have been the last British attempt to sail the Northwest Passage, and success seemed assured for most of the route had already been explored. Franklin's orders were to sail west through Lancaster Sound, to Cape Walker off northern Prince of Wales Island, and then south through Peel Sound. If he was stopped by ice in Barrow Strait he was to try to sail north through Wellington Channel.

The *Erebus* and *Terror* crossed the north Atlantic without mishap and sailed north along the west coast of Greenland. On July 19th they fell in with whalers off Upernavik and Franklin talked with the masters of the ships at length about ice conditions in Baffin Bay. He wrote a long letter to Edward Parry, to be sent to England on one of the whaling ships. On July 26th the *Erebus* and *Terror* were seen by another whaler at latitude seventy-four degrees forty-eight minutes, waiting for a chance to get through the ice of northern Baffin Bay. On the morning of July 27th, 1845, they were gone. No one but Eskimo hunters ever saw them again.

It was five years after the ships left England that the first trace of the expedition was found, on Beechey Island in Lancaster Sound. Captain Ommaney, of the search expedition commanded by Captain Austin, found signs of a camp which indicated that Sir John and his men had spent the winter of 1845-6 in their frozen-in ships at what is now Erebus Bay on the southwest corner of Devon Island. Tracks seen on gravel beaches indicated the men had made a short sled trip, hauling very heavy loads, along the nearby shore of Wellington Channel. A leather glove left to dry under a rock and not picked up, plus other articles left scattered on the shore, indicated a hasty departure, perhaps as the ships were suddenly released from the ice in the bay. Graves told of three deaths among the crews that first winter away from home but, search as they would, they could find no written record, nothing to tell of the expedition to that date, nothing to tell of the intentions for the future.

In 1853, eight years after Franklin's ships had left the shores of England, and after dozens of ships had combed the sea lanes among many of the Arctic Islands without finding any trace of Franklin's ships or his men, Dr. John Rae of the Hudson's Bay Company was sent on a search expedition by land northwest from Hudson Bay. This was his second overland trip to the northeast coast of Melville Peninsula. In 1846-7 he had wintered at Repulse Bay, the first overland explorer ever to winter on the north coast, while he charted the coasts of Committee

Bay. At one point on this trip, quite unknown to him, he had been within 250 miles of the place where Franklin's ships were trapped in the ice of Victoria Strait. Rae spent the winter of 1853-4 at Repulse Bay, then set off for Boothia Peninsula in the spring. On this trip he made the discovery that King William "Land" was an island, separated from Boothia by a narrow, shallow strait, now named after himself. The correction to the charts came eight years too late for John Franklin.

On the west coast of Boothia Peninsula Rae met Eskimos who told him that they had never seen white men before, but they had heard of a party all of whom died of starvation a long distance to the west, beyond a large river. From the Eskimos Rae purchased many articles—silver forks and spoons, an Order of Merit in the form of a star, a small silver plate engraved with the words "Sir John Franklin, K.C.B." Rae returned to England to report on what he had found, the first man to bring reports and relics of the lost expedition.

Five more years passed before Captain Leopold M'Clintock, leading a search expedition financed by Lady Franklin and friends, found positive proof of the death of Sir John and many of his men. From his ship, the *Fox,* frozen in the ice at the eastern end of Bellot Strait, M'Clintock and a Greenlander interpreter, Carl Peterson, travelled by dogs and sled along the west coast of Boothia Peninsula in the late winter of 1859. Not far from the site of the North Magnetic Pole, found by J.C. Ross in 1831, M'Clintock came upon a winter camp of Eskimo hunters. From them he learned that two big ships had been frozen-in among the ice of Victoria Strait off the northern tip of King William Island. One ship had been nipped by the ice and had sunk, but the other had been boarded by the Eskimos who found and ransacked her.

I purchased from them six pieces of silver plate, bearing the crests or initials of Franklin, Crozier, Fairholme, and M'Donald; they also sold us bows and arrows of English woods, uniform and other buttons, and offered us a heavy sledge made of two stout pieces of curved wood, which no mere boat could have furnished them with. . . . They told us it was five days journey to the wreck—one day up the inlet still in sight, and four days overland; this would carry them to the western coast of King William "Land"; they added that but little remained of the wreck which was accessible, their countrymen having carried almost everything away. In answer to an inquiry they said she was without masts; the question gave rise to some laughter amongst them, and they spoke to each other about fire, from which Peterson thought they had burnt the masts through close to the deck in order to get them down. There had been many books, they said, but all have long since been destroyed by the weather; the ship was forced on shore in the fall by ice. She had not been visited during the last winter, and an old woman and a boy were shown to us who were the last to visit the wreck.[1]

M'Clintock's second in command, Lieutenant Hobson, travelling by sled down the west coast of King William Island, came upon a stone cairn at Victory Point. In the cairn was a record from the Franklin expedition, the only one ever to be found, written on a regulation Admiralty form:

28 of May, 1847. H.M. Ships Erebus and Terror wintered in ice at 70° 05′ N., long. 98° 23′ W.[2] Having wintered in 1846-47[3] at Beechey Island in lat. 74° 43′ 28″ N. long. 91° 39′ 15″ W. after having ascended Wellington Channel to lat. 77° and returned by West side of Cornwallis Island.
Sir John Franklin commanding the Expedition
All Well.

---

[1] L. M'Clintock, *The Voyage of the 'Fox' in Arctic Seas* (London: Murray, 1859), pp. 260-2.

[2] A few miles northwest of Cape Felix, King William Island

[3] An error in dating. It should read 1845-6.

a

b

Old and new

Overleaf/C.C.G.S. *d'Iberville,* one of Canada's fleet of
modern icebreakers, easily steams through
the rotting ice of Eureka Sound in the High
Arctic in summer.

a/ Icebergs still pose a threat to ships in the
Arctic sea lanes. More than three-quarters
of the bulk of the iceberg is invisible below
the surface.

b/ Modern re-supply operations in the Arctic:
icebreakers, ice-strengthened ships and
landing barges combine to bring supplies in
summer to Hall Lake DEW Line site.

c/ A few descendants of early Eskimo hunters
still live and hunt on the north coast of
Canada near Pelly Bay and Chantrey Inlet.

d/ An Eskimo housewife talks with a neighbour,
or with a relative in southern Canada, from
her modern wooden house at the new town
of Frobisher Bay.

e/ Skills of the Eskimo of old: clothes tailored
from caribou skins and a sled made from
frozen fish, sealskin and caribou antlers.

c

d

e

Twentieth-century man comes to the Arctic

a/ A National Film Board movie crew is filming
scenes of seal hunting for the award winning
documentary film on Eskimo life, "Land of
the Long Day," on north Baffin Island, April
1951.

b/ Modern transportation in the Arctic: the
bush plane on skis or floats is still the
workhorse of the North.

c/ Heavy ice clogs Hudson Strait today, just as
it did almost 400 years ago when Frobisher
and Hudson sailed this way.

c

d/ C.C.G.S. icebreaker, *John A. Macdonald,*   e
goes to the rescue of a cargo ship caught
in heavy Arctic ice floes.

e/ An oversnow vehicle of the Canadian Army
"Operation Musk Ox," on Great Bear Lake.
It is *en route* to Edmonton in the spring of
1946 after crossing the Arctic Barrens from
Churchill to Cambridge Bay.

d

a

b

c

Doug Wilkinson in the Arctic

a/ Doug in his kayak on north Baffin Island, while living as an Eskimo hunter for a year (1953-4).

b/ Doug looking out over the Barrens, with his camera on the rock beside him, as he explored part of Hearne's route to the north coast.

c/ Doug on his first trip to the Arctic in the winter of 1945-6, standing atop one of the vehicles of "Operation Musk Ox" before taking off on an expedition from old Fort Churchill on Hudson Bay.

Modern communication and transportation

a/ Radome and communication antennae of a DEW Line site on the north coast are the eyes and ears of a modern communications system and network of airfields across the coast of Arctic Canada.

b/ The town and port of Churchill on Hudson Bay — Canada's only Arctic seaport with direct rail connection to the south. The Churchill River, grain elevator and dock are in the foreground, while Hudson Bay and the town are in the background.

a

b

Party consisting of 2 officers and 6 men left the ships on Monday, 24th. May 1847.

Gm Gore Lieut.
Chas F Des Voeuz Mate.[4]

Around the margins of this note had been added another message, written one year later when all was not well.

In 1848, H.M. Ships Terror and Erebus were deserted on the 22nd April 5 leagues N.N.W. of this, having been beset since 12 Sept. 1846, the officers and crews consisting of 105 souls under the command of Captain F.R.M. Crozier landed here in Lat. 69° 37′ 42″ and Long. 98° 41′. This paper was found by Lieut. Irving under the cairn supposed to have been built by Sir James Ross in 1831 4 miles to the northward where it had been deposited by the late Commander Gore in June, 1847. Sir James Ross's pillar has not however been found, and the paper has been transferred to this position, which is that in which Sir J. Ross's pillar was erected—Sir John Franklin died on the 11th June, 1847, and the total loss by deaths in the Expedition has been to this date 9 officers and 15 men.

James Fitzjames, Captain,
H.M.S. Erebus

F.R.M. Crozier
Captain and Senior Officer
And start on to-morrow 26th for Back's Fish River.[5]

The pattern was clear. Franklin had sailed south through Peel Sound and Franklin Strait.[6] Off the northern tip of King William Island he came up against the edge of the main ice

---

[4] L. M'Clintock, *The Voyage of . . .* , facing p. 283.
[5] *Ibid.*
[6] The late Henry Larsen was of the opinion that Franklin had sailed north of Prince of Wales Island and down M'Clintock Channel where he was caught in the heavy ice.

stream down M'Clintock Channel. His charts showed King William "Land" connected to the mainland across what is in fact Rae Strait. There was apparently no opening through in that direction. Besides, that way led southeast and it was to the southwest that he wished to go. With the season well-advanced, with new ice forming on the water, he took his ships into the massive, polar ice of Victoria Strait. They never moved under their own power again.

In 1848, with Franklin dead and his men suffering from scurvy after three winters in the Arctic ice, Crozier had ordered the ships abandoned. The survivors landed on King William Island at Victory Point and began their long march south, hoping to reach the Back River and ascend it to the nearest fur-trade post on Great Slave Lake. None made it, but, by marching down the coast of King William Island to Simpson Strait, some of their number became the first men from western Europe to cross the unknown central section of one of the waterways across northern North America. They paid for this honour with their lives.

Near Cape John Herschel, on the south coast of King William Island, M'Clintock came upon a skeleton still partially clothed in wind-tattered rags that had once been the uniform of a naval rating. The man had fallen face down as he walked south. He died alone and unattended.

> Peterson questioned the woman closely, and she seemed anxious to give all the information in her power. She said many of the white men dropped by the way as they went to the Great River; that some were buried and some were not.[7]

On the west coast of Graham Gore Peninsula, M'Clintock found a ship's boat mounted on an enormous, heavy sledge. Inside the boat were two skeletons, and relics such as watches, silverware and shotguns. The boat was equipped with paddles, not oars, ready for the hoped-for ascent of the Back River and

[7] L. M'Clintock, *The Voyage of . . .* , p. 262.

safety in the south. He saw no sign of the wreck described by the Eskimos and assumed that it had sunk in Victoria Strait.

Other searchers found more skeletons and relics of the grim march down the west coast of King William Island and onto the mainland at Adelaide Peninsula. In 1869, Charles Francis Hall found portions of a skeleton on Todd Island in Simpson Strait, as well as another skeleton, later identified as that of Lieutenant Le Vescomte. From the Eskimos he heard of an encampment they had found at the head of Terror Bay: one large tent inside of which were blankets, utensils, pistols, ammunition and books, around which lay human bones in disarray. From the Eskimos he purchased many relics, including a tiny, mahogany writing desk, eighteen inches long by ten inches wide. From them he heard of the remains of men found with arms and legs cut by saws, as if the survivors had been driven to the horrible extremity of cannibalism in their last desperate efforts to stay alive.

Lieutenant Frederick Schwatka of the United States Army came to King William Island in the spring of 1879, travelling by dogs and sled from the west coast of Hudson Bay at Chesterfield Inlet. He found graves near Victory Point and, not far away, discovered the site of the camp where the crews had come ashore after the abandonment of the ships. The ground was littered with items hauled ashore and then left behind when the men started south—stoves, kettles, blankets, clothing. He found a silver medal, the prize for mathematics won by Lieutenant John Irving at the Royal Naval College in 1830, as well as a brush with the name H. Wilks engraved on it. Near Cape Sydney he found a cairn which had been partly dismantled. Beneath a stone near the top he found a fragment of paper on which was the drawing of a hand, pointing.

In 1923 the great Knud Rasmussen, on his epic sled trip across northern North America from Greenland to Alaska, heard from an old Eskimo hunter, Iggiarjuk, the story of the last days of some of Franklin's men.

My father, Mangnak, was out with Terqatsaq and Qavdlut hunting seal on the west coast of King William Island, when they heard shouts, and perceived three white men standing on the shore and beckoning to them. This was in the spring, there was already open water along the shore, and they could not get in to where the others stood until low water. The white men were very thin, with sunken cheeks, and they looked ill; they wore the clothes of white men, and had no dogs, but pulled the sledge themselves. They bought some seal meat and blubber, and gave a knife in payment. There was much rejoicing on both sides over the trade; the white men at once boiled the meat with some of the blubber and ate it. Then they came home to my father's tent and stayed the night, returning the next day to their own tent, which was small and not made of skins, but of something as white as snow. There were already caribou at that season, but the strangers seemed to hunt only birds. The eider duck and ptarmigan were plentiful, but the earth had not yet come to life, and the swans had not yet arrived. My father and those with him would gladly have helped the white men, but could not understand their speech; they tried to explain by signs, and in this way much was learned. It seemed that they had formerly been many, but now they were few, and their ship was left out on the ice. They pointed towards the south, and it was understood that they proposed to return to their own place overland. Afterwards, no more was seen of them, and it was not known what had become of them.[8]

One hundred and five officers and men of the British Navy died along the snow-covered beaches over which I flew on that day in April 1962. Names on my map told the story of some of the brave men who perished on the coasts of King William Island and the nearby mainland; Cape Francis Crozier, named after the second in command of the expedition, who succeeded as commander after Franklin died on board his frozen-in ship,

[8] Knud Rasmussen, *Across Arctic America* (New York: Putnam, 1927), pp. 172-3.

and who led his men south during that horrible spring and summer of 1848; Graham Gore Peninsula, after a lieutenant on board the *Erebus,* a veteran of other expeditions to the Arctic who also died on his ship before the long march began; Le Vesconte Point, in memory of Lieutenant Le Vescomte, a young friend of Franklin whose skeleton was found on a lonely beach by Hall, who sent it to England for burial; Irving Island, after Lieutenant John Irving of the *Terror,* whose grave was found near Victory Point by Lieutenant Schwatka, who sent the remains to Irving's relatives in Scotland. Erebus Bay and Terror Bay commemorate the two ships lost. Two Grave Bay is an eloquent reminder of a searcher's findings on a lonely shore.

For long moments I gazed down at the snow-covered land and sea passing slowly beneath the plane. I'd done enough Arctic sled travel under poor conditions and short rations to know something of the plight of these desperate, starving men, all suffering from the physical and mental depression of the dreaded disease scurvy, slowly hauling their heavily-laden sledges down the bleak coast below. Their plan for escape was hopeless from the beginning. I wondered how many of the officers knew this before they started out. Some must have known. The ship's boat, found by Hobson mounted on a sled, was pointed north, in the direction of the frozen-in ships, as though some of the men had decided to give up the hopeless march to the south and return to the only refuge they knew.

The coast of King William Island passed beneath the port wing of the plane and I reported to the DEW Line station at Gladman Point. The voice of the operator came back calm and clear. I wondered if he ever thought of those days of long ago when starving, dying men dragged themselves over the rotting ice of Simpson Strait, only a mile or two from where he lived in comfort. Probably not. It all happened so long ago, and we forget so easily.

As this thought passed through my mind, I made a sudden

decision. A quick check of the fuel remaining on board showed there would be enough for a detour, if I didn't linger too long. Banking the plane right I flew southeast for about fifteen minutes to the north coast of Adelaide Peninsula, then let down to fly about 500 feet above the ground. Below, the low, snow-covered coast was difficult to see in the white glare, but I found the faint outline of the shore I sought. On my map it was called Starvation Cove, and the name fits well. Here the last survivors of the Franklin march came to their final resting place: forty desperate, dying men, driven to the horrible extreme of cannibalism as they tried by every means possible to keep the flame of life flickering. None succeeded. All died. One or two may have struggled inland for a few miles. It is possible that one or two may have lived with Eskimo hunters for a few months. But eventually they all died, to lie alone and uncovered on the shores of the Arctic sea channel they had come so far to find. In the final camp at Starvation Cove some one of the group must have been the last to go who, "after the death of his last remaining companions, was all alone in that terrible world, gazing about him in mute despair, the sole living thing in that dark, desolate universe."[9]

I circled slowly above, then suddenly swung the plane wide, away from the ice and snow-covered cove. Banking sharply I came back, fast and low, rocking the wings in salute to the brave men who died here so long ago. As I pulled up and headed north a quick picture flashed through my mind: Knud Rasmussen, on his sled trip across the top of America, standing with head bowed and bared on the shore of Starvation Cove in 1923, the first man to come here since the deaths of Franklin's men, reading the burial service over the scattered remains of the gallant seamen, while the ensigns of Great Britain and Denmark flew at half-staff on makeshift poles set up on the shore of the bay.

[9] Sir Allen Young, *Cruise of the Pandora* (London: W. Clowes and Sons, 1876).

Yes, I am troubled as I write about Sir John Franklin, as I try to see him clearly. For I discern a pattern that seems to run through much of his adult life. On his first expedition to Arctic Canada Franklin led his men to the north coast and east to Kent Peninsula. Showing great personal courage and example, he led them on their terrible retreat to Fort Enterprise. But, in the end, he led them to almost total disaster. Sheer luck saved Franklin and all his men from dying of starvation and cold. As it was, eleven of twenty men on the expedition died horribly in the northern bush. In Tasmania, in an episode far removed from the Arctic coast, Franklin allowed a situation, in which he was the leader, to deteriorate to the point where he was dismissed and recalled by his superiors. Finally, he led his third expedition to the Arctic, where he and 129 men and two ships seemed to vanish as from the face of the earth.

In each case there were mitigating circumstances for the disgrace or disaster, but the fact remains that of the five episodes of his adult life—first expedition to the Arctic coast, second expedition to the Arctic coast, naval service in the Mediterranean, Lieutenant-Governor of Tasmania, third expedition to the Arctic coast—three ended in some measure of major misfortune, while the final one resulted in death for himself and his companions. No other early Arctic explorer in North America, many of whom encountered difficulties as great as those of Sir John Franklin, suffered the major, recurring disasters with which he seemed afflicted. It is this pattern that troubles me as I write.

Leadership calls for exceptional abilities in an individual. He or she must be aware constantly of what has happened, of what is happening, and of what is most likely to happen as a result of actions taken in past and present. A leader must not only have qualities of great personal courage and skill. He must also have that extra quality of being able to stand aside of a situation in such a way that he sees, as if with a third eye, coldly, clearly, objectively, the options that are open to him and various results which will likely accompany these. In my view Martin Frobisher had this quality. So did Samuel Hearne and Edward Parry. In my view John Franklin did not have it, despite all the other excellent qualities he possessed, and this was the fundamental cause of the misfortunes he suffered on the Coppermine River, in Tasmania, and in the ice off King William Island. Because he didn't have it 140 men under his command died horribly to lie in unknown and unmarked graves in northern Canada.

Human life is far too precious to be squandered for limited goals and, in the mid-nineteenth century, the discovery of the Northwest Passage held little significance for the world. The British naval officers who commanded the voyages of exploration to the North American Arctic sought honour and glory, for themselves and for England. The sacrifice of human life to honour and glory may be worthwhile if the individual or small group in question wishes to take a chance. But no amount of honour or glory can be worth the lives of 140 men, most of whom had little stake in the possible rewards at the end of the rainbow.

Suppose we say they sought truth, not only honour and glory. True knowledge, the ultimate goal of all scientific endeavour, including geographic discovery. The search for truth occasionally requires great sacrifice, often the ultimate sacrifice of those engaged in the search. But truth about the coastal outlines of northern North America in the mid-nineteenth century was hardly worth the sacrifice of the 140 men who died of disease, cold and starvation along the desolate shores to which they had come. Fridtjof Nansen, a great humanist and Arctic explorer,[10] had this to say about the Arctic land to which he had come in search of truth:

[10] He sought to drift across the Arctic Ocean in his ship the *Fram*, which was frozen into the ice of the central pack. He kept a journal while on board.

Oh, how tired I am of thy cold beauty! I long to return to life. Let me go home again, as conqueror or beggar; what does it matter? But let me get home to begin life anew. The years are passing here, and what do they bring? Nothing but dust, dry dust, which the first wind blows away; new dust comes in to take its place, and the next wind takes it too. Truth? Why should we always make so much of truth? Life is more than cold truth, and we live but once.[11]

[11] F. Nansen, *Farthest North* (London: Chatto & Windus, 1897), p. 309.

Epilogue

Men from Great Britain found the last links of the Northwest Passage water routes across the top of America. Franklin's men walked over the ice of Victoria Strait. John Rae discovered Rae Strait. In 1852 Robert M'Clure walked across the ice of Prince of Wales Strait to the south shore of Melville Sound, to connect his discoveries with those of Edward Parry. In 1853 M'Clure and his men left their ship the *Investigator* frozen into the ice of Mercy Bay on northern Banks Island, and walked across the ice of M'Clure Strait and Viscount Melville Sound, to become the first men from western Europe to travel the Northwest Passage.

Fifty more years passed before the first ship sailed along its length. That honour went to a tiny ex-fishing vessel, the *Gjoa*, captained by a Norwegian, Roald Amundsen, who later beat England's Robert Scott and became the first man to stand at the true South Pole. In 1903, Amundsen sailed from Norway, leaving in the dead of night to escape angry creditors it is said. He sailed through Lancaster Sound, Barrow Strait, Peel Sound and Franklin Strait, then around behind King William Island through the waters of Rae Strait and, after wintering three times in Arctic ice, sailed on to the open waters of the Pacific

Ocean. Three hundred and thirty-one years after Martin Frobisher sailed into his "Streightes" on southern Baffin Island, a sailing ship managed to complete the task begun so many years before.

The early Arctic explorers were not Canadians. Canada did not exist in their time. They had no visions of a great northern nation in America. They sought knowledge, wealth, honour and glory. Yet, in the wider view, they were all Canadians, fellow members of a nation yet unborn in their time. We of later ages are forever in their debt. Whether we are Eskimo, Indian or Caucasian, we can look back with pride at the part played by many of our ancestors in the discovery and development of the Arctic regions of our land. To them, and to them alone, we are indebted for a Canada that stretches not only east and west from Atlantic to Pacific, but also reaches out north, to the ice-covered waters of the polar sea.

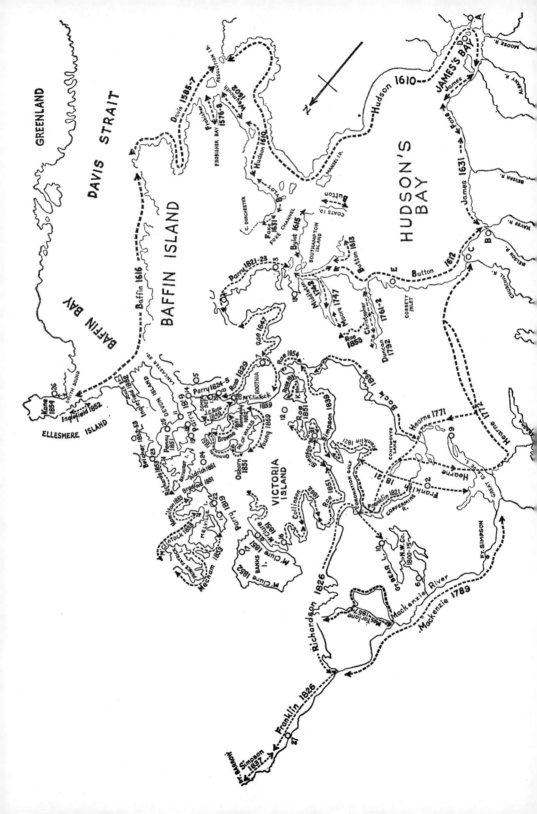

Index